ESSAYS ON BUSINESS AND MANAGEMENT

ESSAYS ON BUSINESS AND MANAGEMENT

Raju Patel

CYBER TECH PUBLICATIONS
4264/3, Ansari Road, Daryaganj, New Delhi-110002 (India)
Ph.: 011-23244078. Fax: 011-23280028
E-Mail: cyberpublicationsdelhi@yahoo.com

Essays on Business and Management

First Edition 2009

Published by G.S. Rawat
For Cyber Tech Publications
4264/3, Ansari Road, Daryaganj, New Delhi-110002
Ph.: 011-23244078. Fax: 011-23280028
E-Mail: cyberpublicationsdelhi@yahoo.com

Printed at
Amit Enterprises, Moujpur, Delhi, Ph. -9810878184

Preface

Most books on Management and Business Studies seem to be written from the point of view of those whose job it is to produce financial statements. They are full of complicated rules and procedures that seem only to confuse those who want to take a more general interest in the subject. This book is not a guide for bookkeepers and others who produce the financial statements. It is for those who will make use of financial accounting. It is particularly directed at those who may be reluctant to tackle the subject, but who can accept that it is not only valuable and useful; it is also a challenging, interesting academic subject, which is directly applicable in the real business world.

The book is intended to help those who produce projects, dissertations and reports, including journalists, who use information about companies: they need to be aware that annual reports and accounts are a valuable source of information, and to be sure that they understand them. It is, in part, a defence of business studies which is intended to show the value, usefulness and applications of the subject. But it is a 'warts and all' presentation which attempts to provide a reasonable exposition of the limitations of financial accounting as well as demonstrating its value and applications. It deals with conventional interpretations of accounts by examining the financial statements of actual companies, not by presenting a series of ratios for students to memorize. It also provides a basis for some of the main issues in financial management, including how to raise additional funds, dividend policy and gearing; working capital management; and investment appraisal.

—Author

CONTENTS

1

INTRODUCTION

Management comprises directing and controlling a group of one or more people or entities for the purpose of coordinating and harmonizing them towards accomplishing a goal. Management often encompasses the deployment and manipulation of human resources, financial resources, technological resources, and natural resources. Management can also refer to the person or people who perform the act(s) of management.

The verb manage comes from the Italian maneggiare (to handle-especially a horse), which in turn derives from the Latin manus (hand). The French word mesnagement (later ménagement) influenced the development in meaning of the English word management in the 17th and 18th centuries.

Management has to do with power by position, whereas leadership involves power by influence. Compare stewardship.

MANAGEMENT FUNCTIONS

Different Levels of Management

Top-level Management

- Top-level managers require an extensive knowledge of management roles and skills.

- They have to be very aware of external factors such as markets.
- Their decisions are generally of a long-term nature.
- They are responsible for strategic decisions.
- They have to chalk out the plan and see that plan may be effective in future.

Middle Management

- Mid-level managers have a specialised understanding of certain managerial tasks.
- They are responsible for and carrying out the decisions made by top-level management.
- They are responsible for tactical decisions.

Lower Management

- This level of management ensures that the decisions and plans taken by the other two are carried out.
- Lower-level managers' decisions are generally short-term ones.

Formation of the Business Policy

- The mission of the business is its most obvious purpose--which may be, for example, to make soap.
- The objective of the business refers to the ends or activity at which a certain task is aimed.
- The business's policy is a guide that stipulates rules, regulations and objectives, and may be used in the managers' decision-making. It must be flexible and easily interpreted and understood by all employees.
- The business's strategy refers to the plan of action that it is going to take, as well as the resources that it will be using, to achieve its mission and objectives. It is a guideline to managers, stipulating how they

ought to use best the factors of production to the business's advantage. Initially, it could help the managers decide on what type of business they want to form.

How to Implement Policies and Strategies

- All policies and strategies must be discussed with all managerial personnel and staff.
- Managers must understand where and how they can implement their policies and strategies.
- A plan of action must be devised for each department.
- Policies and strategies must be reviewed regularly.
- Contingency plans must be devised in case the environment changes.
- Assessments of progress ought to be carried out regularly by top-level managers.
- A good environment is required within the business.

The Development of Policies and Strategies

- The missions, objectives, strengths and weaknesses of each department must be analysed to determine their roles in achieving the business's mission.
- The forecasting method develops a reliable picture of the business's future environment.
- A planning unit must be created to ensure that all plans are consistent and that policies and strategies are aimed at achieving the same mission and objectives.
- Contingency plans must be developed, just in case.

All policies must be discussed with all managerial personnel and staff that is required in the execution of any departmental policy.

Where Policies and Strategies fit into the Planning Process

- They give mid-and lower-level managers a good idea of the future plans for each department.
- A framework is created whereby plans and decisions are made.
- Mid-and lower-level management may add their own plans to the business's strategic ones.

BASIC FUNCTIONS OF MANAGEMENT

Management operates through various functions, often classified as planning, organizing, leading/motivating and controlling.

- Planning: deciding what needs to happen in the future (today, next week, next month, next year, over the next five years, etc.) and generating plans for action.
- Organizing: making optimum use of the resources required to enable the successful carrying out of plans.
- Leading/Motivating: exhibiting skills in these areas for getting others to play an effective part in achieving plans.
- Controlling: monitoring--checking progress against plans, which may need modification based on feedback.

Theoretical Scope

Mary Parker Follett (1868-1933), who wrote on the topic in the early twentieth century, defined management as "the art of getting things done through people". One can also think of management functionally, as the action of measuring a quantity on a regular basis and of adjusting some initial plan; or as the actions taken to reach one's intended goal.

This applies even in situations where planning does not take place. From this perspective, Frenchman Henri Fayol considers management to consist of five functions:

1. planning
2. organizing
3. leading
4. co-ordinating
5. controlling

Some people, however, find this definition, while useful, far too narrow. The phrase "management is what managers do" occurs widely, suggesting the difficulty of defining management, the shifting nature of definitions, and the connection of managerial practices with the existence of a managerial cadre or class.

One habit of thought regards management as equivalent to "business administration", although this then excludes management in places outside commerce, as for example in charities and in the public sector. Nonetheless, many people refer to university departments which teach management as "business schools." Some institutions (such as the Harvard Business School) use that name while others (such as the Yale School of Management) employ the more inclusive term "management."

Speakers of English may also use the term "management" or "the management" as a collective word describing the managers of an organization, for example of a corporation. Historically this use of the term was often contrasted with the term "Labor" referring to those being managed.

HISTORICAL DEVELOPMENT

Difficulties arise in tracing the history of management. Some see it (by definition) as a late modern (in the sense of late modernity) conceptualization. On those terms it cannot have a pre-modern history, only harbingers (such as stewards). Others, however, detect management-like activities in the pre-modern past. Some writers [Who?] trace the development of management-thought back to Sumerian traders and to the builders of the pyramids of ancient Egypt. Slave-owners through the centuries faced the problems of exploiting/motivating a dependent but sometimes unenthusiastic or recalcitrant workforce, but many pre-industrial enterprises, given their small scale, did not feel compelled to face the issues of management systematically. However, innovations such as the spread of Hindu-Arabic numerals (5th to 15th centuries) and the codification of double-entry book-keeping (1494) provided tools for management assessment, planning and control.

Given the scale of most commercial operations and the lack of mechanized record-keeping and recording before the industrial revolution, it made sense for most owners of enterprises in those times to carry out management functions by and for themselves. But with growing size and complexity of organizations, the split between owners (individuals, industrial dynasties or groups of shareholders) and day-to-day managers (independent specialists in planning and control) gradually became more common.

19th Century

Some argue that modern management as a discipline began as an off-shoot of economics in the 19th century. Classical economists such as Adam Smith (1723-1790) and John Stuart Mill (1806-1873) provided a theoretical background to resource-allocation, production, and pricing issues.

About the same time, innovators like Eli Whitney (1765-1825), James Watt (1736-1819), and Matthew Boulton (1728-1809) developed elements of technical production such as standardization, quality-control procedures, cost-accounting, interchangeability of parts, and work-planning. Many of these aspects of management existed in the pre-1861 slave-based sector of the US economy. That environment saw 4 million people, as the contemporary usages had it, "managed" in profitable quasi-mass production.

By the late 19th century, marginal economists Alfred Marshall (1842-1924) and Léon Walras (1834-1910) and others introduced a new layer of complexity to the theoretical underpinnings of management. Joseph Wharton offered the first tertiary-level course in management in 1881.

20th Century

By about 1900 one finds managers trying to place their theories on what they regarded as a thoroughly scientific basis (see scientism for perceived limitations of this belief). Examples include Henry R. Towne's Science of management in the 1890s, Frederick Winslow Taylor's Scientific management (1911), Frank and Lillian Gilbreth's Applied motion study (1917), and Henry L. Gantt's charts (1910s). J. Duncan wrote the first college management textbook in 1911. In 1912 Yoichi Ueno introduced Taylorism to Japan and became first management consultant of the "Japanese-management style". His son Ichiro Ueno pioneered Japanese quality-assurance.

The first comprehensive theories of management appeared around 1920. The Harvard Business School invented the Master of Business Administration degree (MBA) in 1921. People like Henri Fayol (1841-1925) and Alexander Church described the various branches of management and their inter-relationships. In the early 20th century, people like Ordway Tead (1891-1973), Walter Scott and J. Mooney applied the principles of psychology to management, while other writers, such as Elton Mayo (1880-1949), Mary Parker Follett (1868-1933), Chester Barnard

(1886-1961), Max Weber (1864-1920), Rensis Likert (1903-1981), and Chris Argyris (1923-) approached the phenomenon of management from a sociological perspective.

Peter Drucker (1909-2005) wrote one of the earliest books on applied management: Concept of the Corporation (published in 1946). It resulted from Alfred Sloan (chairman of General Motors until 1956) commissioning a study of the organisation. Drucker went on to write 39 books, many in the same vein.

H. Dodge, Ronald Fisher (1890-1962), and Thornton C. Fry introduced statistical techniques into management-studies. In the 1940s, Patrick Blackett combined these statistical theories with microeconomic theory and gave birth to the science of operations research. Operations research, sometimes known as "management science" (but distinct from Taylor's scientific management), attempts to take a scientific approach to solving management problems, particularly in the areas of logistics and operations.

Some of the more recent developments include the Theory of Constraints, management by objectives, reengineering, and various information-technology-driven theories such as agile software development, as well as group management theories such as Cog's Ladder.

As the general recognition of managers as a class solidified during the 20th century and gave perceived practitioners of the art/science of management a certain amount of prestige, so the way opened for popularised systems of management ideas to peddle their wares. In this context many management fads may have had more to do with pop psychology than with scientific theories of management.

Towards the end of the 20th century, business management came to consist of six separate branches, namely:

- Human resource management
- Operations management or production management
- Strategic management
- Marketing management
- Financial management
- Information technology management responsible for management information systems

21st Century

In the 21st century observers find it increasingly difficult to subdivide management into functional categories in this way. More and more processes simultaneously involve several categories. Instead, one tends to think in terms of the various processes, tasks, and objects subject to management.

Branches of management theory also exist relating to nonprofits and to government: such as public administration, public management, and educational management. Further, management programs related to civil-society organizations have also spawned programs in nonprofit management and social entrepreneurship.

Note that many of the assumptions made by management have come under attack from business ethics viewpoints, critical management studies, and anti-corporate activism.

As one consequence, workplace democracy has become both more common, and more advocated, in some places distributing all management functions among the workers, each of whom takes on a portion of the work. However, these models predate any current political issue, and may occur more naturally than does a command hierarchy. All management to some degree embraces democratic principles in that in the long term workers must give majority support to management; otherwise they leave to find other work, or go on strike. Hence management has started to become less based on the conceptualisation of classical military command-and-control, and more about facilitation and support of collaborative activity, utilizing principles such as those of human interaction management to deal with the complexities of human interaction. Indeed, the concept of Ubiquitous command-and-control posits such a transformation for 21st century military management.

Nature of Managerial Work

In for-profit work, management has as its primary function the satisfaction of a range of stakeholders. This typically involves making a profit (for the shareholders), creating valued products at a reasonable cost (for customers), and providing rewarding employment opportunities (for employees). In nonprofit management, add the importance of keeping the faith of donors. In most models of management/ governance, shareholders vote for the board of directors, and the board then hires senior management. Some organizations have experimented with other methods (such as employee-voting models) of selecting or reviewing managers; but this occurs only very rarely.

In the public sector of countries constituted as representative democracies, voters elect politicians to public office. Such politicians hire many managers and administrators, and in some countries like the United States political appointees lose their jobs on the election of a new president/governor/mayor. Some 2500 people serve at the pleasure of the United States Chief Executive, including all of the top US government executives.

Public, private, and voluntary sectors place different demands on managers, but all must retain the faith of those who select them (if they wish to retain their jobs), retain the faith of those people that fund the organization, and retain the faith of those who work for the organization. If they fail to convince employees of the advantages of staying rather than leaving, they may tip the organization into a downward spiral of hiring, training, firing, and recruiting. Management also has the task of innovating and of improving the functioning of organizations.

HUMAN RESOURCES

Human resources is a human that gives information about knowlegde and other interesting things, employee relations and resource planning. The field draws upon concepts developed in Industrial/Organizational Psychology. Human resources has at least two related interpretations depending on context. The original usage derives from political economy and economics, where it was traditionally called labor, one of four factors of production. The more common usage within corporations and businesses refers to the individuals within the firm, and to the portion of the firm's organization that deals with hiring, firing, training, and other personnel issues. This article addresses both definitions.

The objective of Human Resources is to maximize the return on investment from the organization's human capital and minimize financial risk. It is the responsibility of human resource managers to conduct these activities in an effective, legal, fair, and consistent manner. Human resource management serves these key functions:

1. Recruitment Strategy Planning
2. Hiring Processes(recruitment)
3. Performance Evaluation and Management
4. Promotions
5. Redundancy
6. Industrial and Employee Relations
7. Record keeping of all personal data.

8. Compensation, pensions, bonuses etc in liaison with Payroll
9. Confidential advice to internal 'customers' in relation to problems at work.

HUMAN RESOURCES

Modern analysis emphasizes that human beings are not "commodities" or "resources", but are creative and social beings that make class contributions beyond 'labor' to a society and to civilization. The broad term human capital has evolved to contain some of this complexity, and in micro-economics the term "firm-specific human capital" has come to represent a meaning of the term "human resources."

Advocating the central role of "human resources" or human capital in enterprises and societies has been a traditional role of Human Resource socialist parties, who claim that value is primarily created by their activity, and accordingly justify a larger claim of profits or relief from these enterprises or societies. Critics say this is just a bargaining tactic which grew out of various practices of medieval European guilds into the modern trade union and collective bargaining unit.

A contrary view, common to capitalist parties, is that it is the infrastructural capital and (what they call) intellectual capital owned and fused by "management" that provides most value in financial capital terms. This likewise justifies a bargaining position and a general view that "human resources" are interchangeable.

A significant sign of consensus on this latter point is the ISO 9000 series of standards which requires a "job description" of every participant in a productive enterprise. In general, heavily unionized nations such as France and Germany have adopted and encouraged such descriptions especially within trade unions. One view of this trend is that a strong social consensus on political economy and a good social welfare system facilitates labor mobility and tends to make the entire economy more productive, as labor can move from one enterprise to another with little controversy or difficulty in adapting.

An important controversy regarding labor mobility illustrates the broader philosophical issue with usage of the phrase "human resources": governments of developing nations often regard developed nations that encourage immigration or "guest workers" as appropriating human capital that is rightfully part of the developing nation and required to further its growth as a civilization. They argue that this appropriation is similar to colonial commodity fiat wherein a colonizing European power would define an arbitrary price for natural resources, extracting which diminished national natural capital.

The debate regarding "human resources" versus human capital thus in many ways echoes the debate regarding natural resources versus natural capital. Over time the United Nations have come to more generally support the developing nations' point of view, and have requested significant offsetting "foreign aid" contributions so that a developing nation losing human capital does not lose the capacity to continue to train new people in trades, professions, and the arts.

An extreme version of this view is that historical inequities such as African slavery must be compensated by current developed nations, which benefited from stolen "human resources" as they were developing. This is an extremely controversial view, but it echoes the general theme of converting human capital to "human resources" and thus greatly diminishing its value to the host society, i.e. "Africa", as it is put to narrow imitative use as "labor" in the using society.

- In a series of reports of the UN Secretary-General to the General Assembly over the last decade [e.g. A/56/162 (2001)], a broad inter sectoral approach to developing human resourcefulness has been outlined as a priority for socio-economic development and particularly anti-poverty strategies. This calls for strategic and integrated public policies, for example in education, health, and employment sectors that promote occupational skills, knowledge and performance enhancement.

In the very narrow context of corporate "human resources", there is a contrasting pull to reflect and require workplace diversity that echoes the diversity of a global customer base. Foreign language and culture skills, ingenuity, humor, and careful listening, are examples of traits that such programs typically require. It would appear that these evidence a general shift to the human capital point of view, and an acknowledgment that human beings do contribute much more to a productive enterprise than "work": they bring their character, their ethics, their creativity, their social connections, and in some cases even their pets and children, and alter the character of a workplace. The term corporate culture is used to characterize such processes.

The traditional but extremely narrow context of hiring, firing, and job description is considered a 20th century anachronism. Most corporate organizations that compete in the modern global economy have adopted a view of human capital that mirrors the modern consensus as above. Some of these, in turn, deprecate the term "human resources" as useless.

As the term refers to predictable exploitations of human capital in one context or another, it can still be said to apply to manual labor, mass agriculture, low skill "McJobs" in service industries, military and other work that has clear job descriptions, and which generally do not encourage creative or social contributions.

In general the abstractions of macro-economics treat it this way-as it characterizes no mechanisms to represent choice or ingenuity. So one interpretation is that "firm-specific human capital" as defined in macro-economics is the modern and correct definition of "human resources"-and that this is inadequate to represent the contributions of "human resources" in any modern theory of political economy.

HUMAN RESOURCE DEVELOPMENT

In terms of recruitment and selection it is important to consider carrying out a thorough job analysis to determine the level of skills/technical abilities, competencies, flexibility of the employee required etc. At this point it is important to consider both the internal and external factors that can have an impact on the recruitment of employees. The external factors are those out-with the powers of the organization and include issues such as current and future trends of the labor market e.g. skills, education level, government investment into industries etc. On the other hand internal influences are easier to control, predict and monitor, for example management styles or even the organizational culture.

In order to know the business environment in which any organization operates, three major trends should be considered:

- Demographics-the characteristics of a population/ workforce, for example, age, gender or social class. This type of trend may have an effect in relation to pension offerings, insurance packages etc.
- Diversity-the variation within the population/ workplace. Changes in society now mean that a larger proportion of organizations are made up of "baby-

boomers" or older employees in comparison to thirty years ago. Also, over recent years organizations have had to become more diverse in their employment practices to cope with the lower work ethic of the newer generations. The service industry for example, has embraced those "baby-boomers" desiring to reenter the workforce. Traditional advocates of "workplace diversity" simply advocate an employee base that is a mirror reflection of the make-up of society in so far as race, gender, sexual orientation, etc. These advocates focus on the social engineering theory without understanding the more important points: diversity of ideas to prevent stagnation of products and business development; expanding the customer base through "outreach"; and profit. Alarmist and advocates of social engineering theory cite a "rise in discrimination, unfair dismissal and sexual/racial harassment cases" as an indicator of the need for more diversity legislation. While such measures have a significant impact on the organization they have little or no real impact on advancing diversity of ideas in the workplace. Anti-discrimination laws and regulations do require businesses to undertake a cost-benifit analysis. The result of this analysis is often to adopt an approach that generally recognizes gender, racial, and sexual orientation diversity as a cheaper alturnative to fighting endless litigation. In summary, diversity, based on social engineering "is about creating a working culture that seeks, respects and values difference" without regard to how diversity increases productive and unity of effort.

- Skills and qualifications-as industries move from manual to a more managerial professions so does the need for more highly skilled graduates. If the market is 'tight' i.e. not enough staff for the jobs, employers will have to compete for employees by offering financial rewards, community investment, etc.

In regard to how individuals respond to the changes in a labour market the following should be understood:

- Geographical spread-how far is the job from the individual? The distance to travel to work should be in line with the pay offered by the organization and the transportation and infrastructure of the area will also be an influencing factor in deciding who will apply for a post.
- Occupational structure-the norms and values of the different careers within an organization. Mahoney 1989 developed 3 different types of occupational structure namely craft (loyalty to the profession), organization career (promotion through the firm) and unstructured (lower/unskilled workers who work when needed).
- Generational difference-different age categories of employees have certain characteristics, for example their behavior and their expectations of the organization.

Recruitment methods are wide and varied, it is important that the job is described correctly and any personal specifications stated. Job recruitment methods can be through job centres, employment agencies/consultants, headhunting, and local/national newspapers. It is important that the correct media is chosen to ensure an appropriate response to the advertised post.

MODERN CONCEPT OF HUMAN RESOURCES

Though human resources have been part of business and organizations since the first days of agriculture, the modern concept of human resources began in reaction to the efficiency focus of Taylorism in the early 1900s. By 1920, psychologists and employment experts in the United States started the human relations movement, which viewed workers in terms of their psychology and fit with companies, rather than as interchangeable parts. This movement grew throughout the middle of the 20th century, placing emphasis on how leadership, cohesion, and loyalty played important roles in organizational success. Although this view was increasingly challenged by more quantitatively rigorous and less "soft" management techniques in the 1960s and beyond, human resources had gained a permanent role within an organization.

HUMAN RESOURCE MANAGEMENT

Human resource management (HRM) is the strategic and coherent approach to the management of an organization's most valued assets-the people working there who individually and collectively contribute to the achievement of the objectives of the business. The terms "human resource management" and "human resources" (HR) have largely replaced the term "personnel management" as a description of the processes involved in managing people in organizations. Human Resource management is evolving rapidly. Human resource management is both an academic theory and a business practice that addresses the theoretical and practical techniques of managing a workforce.

Synonyms

Its synonyms include:

- Personnel administration
- Personnel management
- Manpower management
- Industrial management

But these traditional expressions are becoming less common for the theoretical discipline. Sometimes even industrial relations and employee relations are confusingly listed as synonyms, although these normally refer to the relationship between management and workers and the behavior of workers in companies.

The theoretical discipline is based primarily on the assumption that employees are individuals with varying goals and needs, and as such should not be thought of as basic business resources, such as trucks and filing cabinets. The field takes a positive view of workers, assuming that virtually all wish to contribute to the enterprise productively, and that the main obstacles to their endeavors are lack of knowledge, insufficient training, and failures of process.

HRM is seen by practitioners in the field as a more innovative view of workplace management than the traditional approach. Its techniques force the managers of an enterprise to express their goals with specificity so that they can be understood and undertaken by the workforce, and to provide the resources needed for them to successfully accomplish their assignments. As such, HRM techniques, when properly practiced, are expressive of the goals and operating practices of the enterprise overall. HRM is also seen by many to have a key role in risk reduction within organistions.

Synonyms such as personnel management are often used in a more restricted sense to describe activities that are necessary in the recruiting of a workforce, providing its members with payroll and benefits, and administrating their work-life needs.

Academic Theory

The goal of human resource management is to help an organization to meet strategic goals by attracting, and maintaining employees and also to manage them effectively. The basic premise of the academic theory of HRM is that humans are not machines, therefore we need to have an interdisciplinary examination of people in the workplace. Fields such as psychology, industrial engineering, industrial and organizational psychology, industrial relations, sociology, and critical theories: postmodernism, post-structuralism play a major role. Many colleges and universities offer bachelor and master degrees in Human Resources Management.

One widely used scheme to describe the role of HRM, developed by Dave Ulrich, defines 4 fields for the HRM function:

- Strategic business partner
- Change agent
- Employee champion
- Administration

However, many HR functions these days struggle to get beyond the roles of administration and employee champion, and are seen rather as reactive than strategically proactive partners for the top management. In addition, HR organizations also have the difficulty in proving how their activities and processes add value to the company. Only in the recent years HR scholars and HR professionals are focusing to develop models that can measure if HR adds value.

CRITICAL ACADEMIC THEORY

Postmodernism plays an important part in Academic Theory and particularly in Critical Theory. Indeed Karen Legge in 'Human Resource Management: Rhetorics and Realities' posses the debate of whether HRM is a modernist project or a postmodern discourse (Legge 2004)? In many ways, critically or not, many writers contend that HRM itself is a movement away from the modernist traditions of personnel (man as machine) towards a postmodernist view of HRM man as individuals. Critiques include the notion that because 'Human' is the subject we should recognise that people are complex and that it is only through various discourses that we understand the world. Man is not Machine, no matter what attempts are made to change it i.e. Fordism / Taylorism, McDonaldisation (Modernism).

Critical Theory also questions whether HRM is the pursuit of "attitudinal shaping" (Wilkinson 1998), particularly when considering empowerment, or perhaps more precisely pseudo-empowerment-as the critical perspective notes.

Business Practice

Human resources management comprises several processes. Together they are supposed to achieve the above mentioned goal. These processes can be performed in an HR department, but some tasks can also be outsourced or performed by line-managers or other departments.

- Workforce planning
- Recruitment (sometimes separated into attraction and selection)
- Induction and Orientation
- Skills management
- Training and development
- Personnel administration
- Compensation in wage or salary
- Time management
- Travel management (sometimes assigned to accounting rather than HRM)

- Payroll (sometimes assigned to accounting rather than HRM)
- Employee benefits administration
- Personnel cost planning
- Performance appraisal

Careers

The sort of careers available in HRM are varied. There are generalist HRM jobs such as human resource assistant. There are careers involved with employment, recruitment and placement and these are usually conducted by interviewers, EEO (Equal Opportunity Employment) specialists or college recruiters. Training and development specialism is often conducted by trainers and orientation specialists. Compensation and benefits tasks are handled by compensation analysts, salary administrators, and benefits administrators.

OPERATIONS MANAGEMENT

Operations management is an area of business that is concerned with the production of goods and services, and involves the responsibility of ensuring that business operations are efficient and effective. It is also the management of resources, the distribution of goods and services to customers, and the analysis of queue systems.

APICS The Association for Operations Management also defines operations management as "the field of study that focuses on the effective planning, scheduling, use, and control of a manufacturing or service organization through the study of concepts from design engineering, industrial engineering, management information systems, quality management, production management, inventory management, accounting, and other functions as they affect the organization" (APICS Dictionary, 11th edition).

Operations also refers to the production of goods and services, the set of value-added activities that transform inputs into many outputs. Fundamentally, these value-adding creative activities should be aligned with market opportunity (see Marketing) for optimal enterprise performance.

Origins

The origins of Operations Management can be traced back to the Industrial Revolution, the same as Scientific Management and Operations Research. Adam Smith treats the topic of the division of labor when opening his 1776 masterpiece: An Inquiry into the Nature and Causes of the Wealth of Nations also commonly known as The Wealth of Nations. The first documented effort to solve operation management issues comes from Eli Withney back in 1798, leading to the birth of the American System of Manufacturers (ASM) by the mid-1800s. It was not until the late 1950's that the scholars noted the importance of vieweing production operations as systems.

Historically, the body of knowledge stemming from industrial engineering formed the basis of the first MBA programs, and is central to operations management as used across diverse business sectors, industry, consulting and non-profit organizations.

Operations Management Planning Criteria

- Control by creating and maintaining a positive flow of work by utilizing what resources and facilities are available
- Lead by developing and cascading the organizations strategy/mission statement to all staff
- Organize resources such as facilities and employees so as to ensure effective production of goods and services

- Plan by prioritizing customer, employee and organizational requirements
- Maintaining and monitoring staffing, levels, Knowledge-Skill-Attitude (KSA), expectations and motivation to fulfill organizational requirements
- Performance Measures for the measurement of performance and consideration of efficiency versus effectiveness

Organizations

The following organizations support and promote operations management

- Institute for Operations Research and the Management Sciences (INFORMS)
- Production and Operations Management Society (POMS)
- The Association for Operations Management (APICS)
- Institute of Operations Management
- Chartered Management Institute
- European Operations Management Association (EurOMA) , which supports the International Journal of Operations & Production Management

STRATEGIC MANAGEMENT

Strategic management is the art and science of formulating, implementing and evaluating cross-functional decisions that will enable an organization to achieve its objectives . It is the process of specifying the organization's objectives, developing policies and plans to achieve these objectives, and allocating resources to implement the policies and plans to achieve the organization's objectives. Strategic management, therefore, combines the activities of the various functional areas of a business to achieve organizational objectives. It is the highest level of managerial activity, usually formulated by the Board of directors and performed by the organization's Chief Executive Officer (CEO) and executive team. Strategic management provides overall direction` to the enterprise and is closely related to the field of Organization Studies.

"Strategic management is an ongoing process that assesses the business and the industries in which the company is involved; assesses its competitors and sets goals and strategies to meet all existing and potential competitors; and then reassesses each strategy annually or quarterly [i.e. regularly] to determine how it has been implemented and whether it has succeeded or needs replacement by a new strategy to meet changed circumstances, new technology, new competitors, a new economic environment., or a new social, financial, or political environment." (Lamb, 1984:ix)

There are Many Software products available in the market that process organisational data and report which aid in Strategic management e.g SAP SEM, SAS..etc

Processes

Strategic management is a combination of three main processes which are as following:

Strategy Formulation

- Performing a situation analysis, self-evaluation and competitor analysis: both internal and external; both micro-environmental and macro-environmental.
- Concurrent with this assessment, objectives are set. This involves crafting vision statements (long term view of a possible future), mission statements (the role that the organization gives itself in society), overall corporate objectives (both financial and

strategic), strategic business unit objectives (both financial and strategic), and tactical objectives.

- These objectives should, in the light of the situation analysis, suggest a strategic plan. The plan provides the details of how to achieve these objectives.

This three-step strategy formulation process is sometimes referred to as determining where you are now, determining where you want to go, and then determining how to get there. These three questions are the essence of strategic planning. SWOT Analysis: I/O Economics for the external factors and RBV for the internal factors.

Strategy Implementation

- Allocation of sufficient resources (financial, personnel, time, technology support)
- Establishing a chain of command or some alternative structure (such as cross functional teams)
- Assigning responsibility of specific tasks or processes to specific individuals or groups
- It also involves managing the process. This includes monitoring results, comparing to benchmarks and best practices, evaluating the efficacy and efficiency of the process, controlling for variances, and making adjustments to the process as necessary.
- When implementing specific programs, this involves acquiring the requisite resources, developing the process, training, process testing, documentation, and integration with (and/or conversion from) legacy processes.

Strategy Evaluation

- Measuring the effectiveness of the organizational strategy.

General Approaches

In general terms, there are two main approaches, which are opposite but complement each other in some ways, to strategic management:

- The Industrial Organizational Approach
    - — based on economic theory-deals with issues like competitive rivalry, resource allocation, economies of scale
    - — assumptions-rationality, self discipline behaviour, profit maximization
- The Sociological Approach

— deals primarily with human interactions

— assumptions-bounded rationality, satisfying behaviour, profit sub-optimality. An example of a company that currently operates this way is Google

Strategic management techniques can be viewed as bottom-up, top-down, or collaborative processes. In the bottom-up approach, employees submit proposals to their managers who, in turn, funnel the best ideas further up the organization. This is often accomplished by a capital budgeting process. Proposals are assessed using financial criteria such as return on investment or cost-benefit analysis. The proposals that are approved form the substance of a new strategy, all of which is done without a grand strategic design or a strategic architect.

The top-down approach is the most common by far. In it, the CEO (such as Don Sheelen, Jeff Bezos and Samuel J. Palmisano) possibly with the assistance of a strategic planning team, decides on the overall direction the company should take. Some organizations are starting to experiment with collaborative strategic planning techniques that recognize the emergent nature of strategic decisions.

The Strategy Hierarchy

In most (large) corporations there are several levels of strategy. Strategic management is the highest in the sense that it is the broadest, applying to all parts of the firm. It gives direction to corporate values, corporate culture, corporate goals, and corporate missions. Under this broad corporate strategy there are often functional or business unit strategies. Functional strategies include marketing strategies, new product development strategies, human resource strategies, financial strategies, legal strategies, supply-chain strategies, and information technology management strategies. The emphasis is on short and medium term plans and is limited to the domain of each department's functional responsibility. Each functional department attempts to do its part in meeting overall corporate objectives, and hence to some extent their strategies are derived from broader corporate strategies.

Many companies feel that a functional organizational structure is not an efficient way to organize activities so they have reengineered according to processes or strategic business units (called SBUs). A strategic business unit is a semi-autonomous unit within an organization. It is usually responsible for its own budgeting, new product decisions, hiring decisions, and price setting. An SBU is treated as an internal profit centre by corporate headquarters. Each SBU is responsible for developing its business strategies, strategies that must be in tune with broader corporate strategies.

The "lowest" level of strategy is operational strategy. It is very narrow in focus and deals with day-to-day operational activities such as scheduling criteria. It must operate within a budget but is not at liberty to adjust or create that budget. Operational level strategy was encouraged by Peter Drucker in his theory of management by objectives (MBO).

Operational level strategies are informed by business level strategies which, in turn, are informed by corporate level strategies. Business strategy, which refers to the aggregated operational strategies of single business firm or that of an SBU in a diversified corporation refers to the way in which a firm competes in its chosen arenas.

Corporate strategy, then, refers to the overarching strategy of the diversified firm. Such corporate strategy answers the questions of "in which businesses should we compete?" and "how does being in one business add to the competitive advantage of another portfolio firm, as well as the competitive advantage of the corporation as a whole?"

Since the turn of the millennium, there has been a tendency in some firms to revert to a simpler strategic structure. This is being driven by information technology. It is felt that knowledge management systems should be used to share information and create common goals. Strategic divisions are thought to hamper this process. Most recently, this notion of strategy has been captured under the rubric of dynamic strategy, popularized by the strategic management textbook authored by Carpenter and Sanders . This work builds on that of Brown and Eisenhart as well as Christensen and portrays firm strategy, both business and corporate, as necessarily embracing ongoing strategic change, and the seamless integration of strategy formulation and implementation. Such change and implementation are usually built into the strategy through the staging and pacing facets.

HISTORICAL DEVELOPMENT OF STRATEGIC MANAGEMENT

Birth of Strategic Management

Strategic management as a discipline originated in the 1950s and 60s. Although there were numerous early contributors to the literature, the most influential pioneers were Alfred D. Chandler, Jr., Philip Selznick, Igor Ansoff, and Peter Drucker.

Alfred Chandler recognized the importance of coordinating the various aspects of management under one all-encompassing strategy. Prior to this time the various functions of management were separate with little overall coordination or strategy. Interactions between functions or between departments were typically handled by a boundary position, that is, there were one or two managers that relayed information back and forth between two departments. Chandler also stressed the importance of taking a long term perspective when looking to the future. In his 1962 groundbreaking work Strategy and Structure, Chandler showed that a long-term coordinated strategy was necessary to give a company structure, direction, and focus. He says it concisely, "structure follows strategy."

In 1957, Philip Selznick introduced the idea of matching the organization's internal factors with external environmental circumstances. This core idea was developed into what we now call SWOT analysis by Learned, Andrews, and others at the Harvard Business School General Management Group. Strengths and weaknesses of the firm are assessed in light of the opportunities and threats from the business environment.

Igor Ansoff built on Chandler's work by adding a range of strategic concepts and inventing a whole new vocabulary. He developed a strategy grid that compared market penetration strategies, product development strategies, market development strategies and horizontal and vertical integration and diversification strategies. He felt that management could use these strategies to systematically prepare for future opportunities and challenges. In his 1965 classic Corporate Strategy, he developed the Gap analysis still used today in which we must understand the gap between where we are currently and where we would like to be, then develop what he called "gap reducing actions".

Peter Drucker was a prolific strategy theorist, author of dozens of management books, with a career spanning five decades. His contributions to strategic management were many but two are most important. Firstly, he stressed the importance of objectives. An organization without clear objectives is like a ship without a rudder. As early as 1954 he was developing a theory of management based on objectives. This evolved into his theory of management by objectives (MBO). According to Drucker, the procedure of setting objectives and monitoring your progress towards them should permeate the entire organization, top to bottom. His other seminal contribution was in predicting the importance of what today we would call intellectual capital. He predicted the rise of what he called the "knowledge worker" and explained the consequences of this for management. He said that knowledge work is non-hierarchical. Work would be carried out in teams with the person most knowledgeable in the task at hand being the temporary leader.

In 1985, Ellen-Earle Chaffee summarized what she thought were the main elements of strategic management theory by the 1970s:

- Strategic management involves adapting the organization to its business environment.
- Strategic management is fluid and complex. Change creates novel combinations of circumstances requiring unstructured non-repetitive responses.
- Strategic management affects the entire organization by providing direction.
- Strategic management involves both strategy formation (she called it content) and also strategy implementation (she called it process).

- Strategic management is partially planned and partially unplanned.
- Strategic management is done at several levels: overall corporate strategy, and individual business strategies.
- Strategic management involves both conceptual and analytical thought processes.

Growth and Portfolio Theory

In the 1970s much of strategic management dealt with size, growth, and portfolio theory. The PIMS study was a long term study, started in the 1960s and lasted for 19 years, that attempted to understand the Profit Impact of Marketing Strategies (PIMS), particularly the effect of market share. Started at General Electric, moved to Harvard in the early 1970s, and then moved to the Strategic Planning Institute in the late 1970s, it now contains decades of information on the relationship between profitability and strategy. Their initial conclusion was unambiguous: The greater a company's market share, the greater will be their rate of profit. The high market share provides volume and economies of scale. It also provides experience and learning curve advantages. The combined effect is increased profits. The studies conclusions continue to be drawn on by academics and companies today: "PIMS provides compelling quantitative evidence as to which business strategies work and don't work"-Tom Peters.

The benefits of high market share naturally lead to an interest in growth strategies. The relative advantages of horizontal integration, vertical integration, diversification, franchises, mergers and acquisitions, joint ventures, and organic growth were discussed. The most appropriate market dominance strategies were assessed given the competitive and regulatory environment.

There was also research that indicated that a low market share strategy could also be very profitable. Schumacher (1973), Woo and Cooper (1982), Levenson (1984), and later Traverso (2002) showed how smaller niche players obtained very high returns.

By the early 1980s the paradoxical conclusion was that high market share and low market share companies were often very profitable but most of the companies in between were not. This was sometimes called the "hole in the middle" problem. This anomaly would be explained by Michael Porter in the 1980s.

The management of diversified organizations required new techniques and new ways of thinking. The first CEO to address the problem of a multi-divisional company was Alfred Sloan at General Motors. GM was decentralized into semi-autonomous "strategic business units" (SBU's), but with centralized support functions.

One of the most valuable concepts in the strategic management of multi-divisional companies was portfolio theory. In the previous decade Harry Markowitz and other financial theorists developed the theory of portfolio analysis. It was concluded that a broad portfolio of financial assets could reduce specific risk. In the 1970s marketers extended the theory to product portfolio decisions and managerial strategists extended it to operating division portfolios. Each of a company's operating divisions were seen as an element in the corporate portfolio. Each operating division (also called strategic business units) was treated as a semi-independent profit center with its own revenues, costs, objectives, and strategies. Several techniques were developed to analyze the relationships between elements in a portfolio. B.C.G. Analysis, for example, was developed by the Boston Consulting Group in the early 1970s. This was the theory that gave us the wonderful image of a CEO sitting on a stool milking a cash cow. Shortly after that the G.E. multi factoral model was developed by General Electric. Companies continued to diversify until the 1980s when it was realized that in many cases a portfolio of operating divisions was worth more as separate completely independent companies.

The Marketing Revolution

The 1970s also saw the rise of the marketing oriented firm. From the beginnings of capitalism it was assumed that the key requirement of business success was a product of high technical quality. If you produced a product that worked well and was durable, it was assumed you would have no difficulty selling them at a profit.

This was called the production orientation and it was generally true that good products could be sold without effort. encapsulated in the saying "Build a better mousetrap and the world will beat a path to your door." This was largely due to the growing numbers of affluent and middle class people that capitalism had created. But after the untapped demand caused by the second world war was saturated in the 1950s it became obvious that products were not selling as easily as they had been. The answer was to concentrate on selling.

The 1950s and 1960s is known as the sales era and the guiding philosophy of business of the time is today called the sales orientation. In the early 1970s Theodore Levitt and others at Harvard argued that the sales orientation had things backward. They claimed that instead of producing products then trying to sell them to the customer, businesses should start with the customer, find out what they wanted, and then produce it for them. The customer became the driving force behind all strategic business decisions. This marketing orientation, in the decades since its introduction, has been reformulated and repackaged under numerous names including customer orientation, marketing philosophy, customer intimacy, customer focus, customer driven, and market focused.

The Japanese Challenge

By the late 70s people had started to notice how successful Japanese industry had become. In industry after industry, including steel, watches, ship building, cameras, autos, and electronics, the Japanese were surpassing American and European companies. Westerners wanted to know why. Numerous theories purported to explain the Japanese success including:

- Higher employee morale, dedication, and loyalty;
- Lower cost structure, including wages;
- Effective government industrial policy;
- Modernization after WWII leading to high capital intensity and productivity;
- Economies of scale associated with increased exporting;
- Relatively low value of the Yen leading to low interest rates and capital costs, low dividend expectations, and inexpensive exports;
- Superior quality control techniques such as Total Quality Management and other systems introduced by W. Edwards Deming in the 1950s and 60s.

Although there was some truth to all these potential explanations, there was clearly something missing. In fact by 1980 the Japanese cost structure was higher than the American. And post WWII reconstruction was nearly 40 years in the past. The first management theorist to suggest an explanation was Richard Pascale.

In 1981 Richard Pascale and Anthony Athos in The Art of Japanese Management claimed that the main reason for

Japanese success was their superior management techniques. They divided management into 7 aspects (which are also known as McKinsey 7S Framework): Strategy, Structure, Systems, Skills, Staff, Style, and Supraordinate goals (which we would now call shared values). The first three of the 7 S's were called hard factors and this is where American companies excelled. The remaining four factors (skills, staff, style, and shared values) were called soft factors and were not well understood by American businesses of the time (for details on the role of soft and hard factors see Wickens P.D. 1995.) Americans did not yet place great value on corporate culture, shared values and beliefs, and social cohesion in the workplace. In Japan the task of management was seen as managing the whole complex of human needs, economic, social, psychological, and spiritual. In America work was seen as something that was separate from the rest of one's life. It was quite common for Americans to exhibit a very different personality at work compared to the rest of their lives. Pascale also highlighted the difference between decision making styles; hierarchical in America, and consensus in Japan. He also claimed that American business lacked long term vision, preferring instead to apply management fads and theories in a piecemeal fashion.

One year later The Mind of the Strategist was released in America by Kenichi Ohmae, the head of McKinsey & Co.'s Tokyo office. (It was originally published in Japan in 1975.) He claimed that strategy in America was too analytical. Strategy should be a creative art: It is a frame of mind that requires intuition and intellectual flexibility. He claimed that Americans constrained their strategic options by thinking in terms of analytical techniques, rote formula, and step-by-step processes. He compared the culture of Japan in which vagueness, ambiguity, and tentative decisions were acceptable, to American culture that valued fast decisions.

Also in 1982 Tom Peters and Robert Waterman released a study that would respond to the Japanese challenge head on. Peters and Waterman, who had several years earlier collaborated with Pascale and Athos at McKinsey & Co. asked "What makes an excellent company?".

They looked at 62 companies that they thought were fairly successful. Each was subject to six performance criteria. To be classified as an excellent company, it had to be above the 50th percentile in 4 of the 6 performance metrics for 20 consecutive years. Forty-three companies passed the test. They then studied these successful companies and interviewed key executives. They concluded in In Search of Excellence that there were 8 keys to excellence that were shared by all 43 firms. They are:

- A bias for action-Do it. Try it. Don't waste time studying it with multiple reports and committees.
- Customer focus-Get close to the customer. Know your customer.
- Entrepreneurship-Even big companies act and think small by giving people the authority to take initiatives.
- Productivity through people-Treat your people with respect and they will reward you with productivity.
- Value oriented CEOs-The CEO should actively propagate corporate values throughout the organization.
- Stick to the knitting-Do what you know well.
- Keep things simple and lean-Complexity encourages waste and confusion.
- Simultaneously centralized and decentralized-Have tight centralized control while also allowing maximum individual autonomy.

The basic blueprint on how to compete against the Japanese had been drawn. But as J.E. Rehfeld (1994) explains it is not a straight forward task due to differences in culture. A certain type of alchemy was required to transform knowledge from various cultures into a management style that allows a specific company to compete in a globally diverse world. He says, for example, that Japanese style kaizen (continuous improvement) techniques, although suitable for people socialized in Japanese culture, have not been successful when implemented in the U.S. unless they are modified significantly.

Gaining Competitive Advantage

The Japanese challenge shook the confidence of the western business elite, but detailed comparisons of the two management styles and examinations of successful businesses convinced westerners that they could overcome the challenge. The 1980s and early 1990s saw a plethora of theories explaining exactly how this could be done. They cannot all be detailed here, but some of the more important strategic advances of the decade are explained below.

Gary Hamel and C. K. Prahalad declared that strategy needs to be more active and interactive; less "arm-chair planning" was needed. They introduced terms like strategic intent and strategic architecture. Their most well known advance was the idea of core competency. They showed how important it was to know the one or two key things that your company does better than the competition.

Active strategic management required active information gathering and active problem solving. In the early days of Hewlett-Packard (H-P), Dave Packard and Bill Hewlett devised an active management style that they called Management By Walking Around (MBWA). Senior H-P managers were seldom at their desks. They spent most of their days visiting employees, customers, and suppliers.

This direct contact with key people provided them with a solid grounding from which viable strategies could be crafted. The MBWA concept was popularized in 1985 by a book by Tom Peters and Nancy Austin. Japanese managers employ a similar system, which originated at Honda, and is sometimes called the 3 G's (Genba, Genbutsu, and Genjitsu, which translate into "actual place", "actual thing", and "actual situation").

Probably the most influential strategist of the decade was Michael Porter. He introduced many new concepts including; 5 forces analysis, generic strategies, the value chain, strategic groups, and clusters. In 5 forces analysis he identifies the forces that shape a firm's strategic environment. It is like a SWOT analysis with structure and purpose. It shows how a firm can use these forces to obtain a sustainable competitive advantage. Porter modifies Chandler's dictum about structure following strategy by introducing a second level of structure: Organizational structure follows strategy, which in turn follows industry structure. Porter's generic strategies detail the interaction between cost minimization strategies, product differentiation strategies, and market focus strategies. Although he did not introduce these terms, he showed the importance of choosing one of them rather than trying to position your company between them. He also challenged managers to see their industry in terms of a value chain. A firm will be successful only to the extent that it contributes to the industry's value chain. This forced management to look at its operations from the customer's point of view. Every operation should be examined in terms of what value it adds in the eyes of the final customer.

In 1993, John Kay took the idea of the value chain to a financial level claiming " Adding value is the central purpose of business activity", where adding value is defined as the difference between the market value of outputs and the cost of inputs including capital, all divided by the firm's net output. Borrowing from Gary Hamel and Michael Porter, Kay claims that the role of strategic management is to identify your core competencies, and then assemble a collection of assets that will increase value added and provide a competitive advantage. He claims that there are 3 types of capabilities that can do this; innovation, reputation, and organizational structure.

The 1980s also saw the widespread acceptance of positioning theory. Although the theory originated with Jack Trout in 1969, it didn't gain wide acceptance until Al Ries and Jack Trout wrote their classic book "Positioning: The Battle For Your Mind" (1979). The basic premise is that a strategy should not be judged by internal company factors but by the way customers see it relative to the competition. Crafting and implementing a strategy involves creating a position in the mind of the collective consumer. Several techniques were applied to positioning theory, some newly invented but most borrowed from other disciplines. Perceptual mapping for example, creates visual displays of the relationships between positions. Multidimensional scaling, discriminant analysis, factor analysis, and conjoint analysis are mathematical techniques used to determine the most relevant characteristics (called dimensions or factors) upon which positions should be based. Preference regression can be used to determine vectors of ideal positions and cluster analysis can identify clusters of positions.

Others felt that internal company resources were the key. In 1992, Jay Barney, for example, saw strategy as assembling the optimum mix of resources, including human, technology, and suppliers, and then configure them in unique and sustainable ways.

Michael Hammer and James Champy felt that these resources needed to be restructured. This process, that they labeled reengineering, involved organizing a firm's assets around whole processes rather than tasks. In this way a team of people saw a project through, from inception to completion. This avoided functional silos where isolated departments seldom talked to each other. It also eliminated waste due to functional overlap and interdepartmental communications.

In 1989 Richard Lester and the researchers at the MIT Industrial Performance Center identified seven best practices and concluded that firms must accelerate the shift away from the mass production of low cost standardized products. The seven areas of best practice were:

- Simultaneous continuous improvement in cost, quality, service, and product innovation
- Breaking down organizational barriers between departments
- Eliminating layers of management creating flatter organizational hierarchies.
- Closer relationships with customers and suppliers
- Intelligent use of new technology
- Global focus
- Improving human resource skills

The search for "best practices" is also called benchmarking. This involves determining where you need to improve, finding an organization that is exceptional in this area, then studying the company and applying its best practices in your firm.

A large group of theorists felt the area where western business was most lacking was product quality. People like W. Edwards Deming, Joseph M. Juran, A. Kearney, Philip Crosby, and Armand Feignbaum suggested quality improvement techniques like Total Quality Management

(TQM), continuous improvement, lean manufacturing, Six Sigma, and Return on Quality (ROQ).

An equally large group of theorists felt that poor customer service was the problem. People like James Heskett (1988), Earl Sasser (1995), William Davidow, Len Schlesinger, A. Paraurgman (1988), Len Berry, Jane Kingman-Brundage, Christopher Hart, and Christopher Lovelock (1994), gave us fishbone diagramming, service charting, Total Customer Service (TCS), the service profit chain, service gaps analysis, the service encounter, strategic service vision, service mapping, and service teams. Their underlying assumption was that there is no better source of competitive advantage than a continuous stream of delighted customers.

Process management uses some of the techniques from product quality management and some of the techniques from customer service management. It looks at an activity as a sequential process. The objective is to find inefficiencies and make the process more effective. Although the procedures have a long history, dating back to Taylorism, the scope of their applicability has been greatly widened, leaving no aspect of the firm free from potential process improvements. Because of the broad applicability of process management techniques, they can be used as a basis for competitive advantage.

Some realized that businesses were spending much more on acquiring new customers than on retaining current ones. Carl Sewell, Frederick Reicheld, C. Gronroos, and Earl Sasser showed us how a competitive advantage could be found in ensuring that customers returned again and again. This has come to be known as the loyalty effect after Reicheld's book of the same name in which he broadens the concept to include employee loyalty, supplier loyalty, distributor loyalty, and shareholder loyalty. They also developed techniques for estimating the lifetime value of a loyal customer, called customer lifetime value (CLV). A significant movement started that attempted to recast selling and marketing techniques into a long term endeavor that created a sustained relationship with customers (called relationship selling, relationship marketing, and customer relationship management). Customer relationship management (CRM) software (and its many variants) became an integral tool that sustained this trend.

James Gilmore and Joseph Pine found competitive advantage in mass customization. Flexible manufacturing techniques allowed businesses to individualize products for each customer without losing economies of scale. This effectively turned the product into a service. They also realized that if a service is mass customized by creating a "performance" for each individual client, that service would be transformed into an "experience". Their book, The Experience Economy, along with the work of Bernd Schmitt convinced many to see service provision as a form of theatre. This school of thought is sometimes referred to as customer experience management (CEM).

Like Peters and Waterman a decade earlier, James Collins and Jerry Porras spent years conducting empirical research on what makes great companies. Six years of research uncovered a key underlying principle behind the 19 successful companies that they studied: They all encourage and preserve a core ideology that nurtures the company. Even though strategy and tactics change daily, the companies, nevertheless, were able to maintain a core set of values. These core values encourage employees to build an organization that lasts. In Built To Last (1994) they claim that short term profit goals, cost cutting, and restructuring will not stimulate dedicated employees to build a great company that will endure. In 2000 Collins coined the term "built to flip" to describe the prevailing business attitudes in Silicon Valley. It describes a business culture where technological change inhibits a long term focus. He also popularized the concept of the BHAG (Big Hairy Audacious Goal). Arie de Geus (1997) undertook a similar study and obtained similar results. He identified four key traits of companies that had prospered for 50 years or more. They are:

- Sensitivity to the business environment-the ability to learn and adjust
- Cohesion and identity-the ability to build a community with personality, vision, and purpose
- Tolerance and decentralization-the ability to build relationships
- Conservative financing

A company with these key characteristics he called a living company because it is able to perpetuate itself. If a company emphasizes knowledge rather than finance, and sees itself as an ongoing community of human being, it has the potential to become great and endure for decades. Such an organization is an organic entity capable of learning (he called it a "learning organization") and capable of creating its own processes, goals, and persona.

Jordan Lewis finds competitive advantage in alliance strategies. Rather than seeing distributors, suppliers, firms in related industries, and even competitors as potential threats or targets for vertical integration, they should be seen as potential assistants or partners. He explains how mutual respect and trust is the cornerstone of this approach and describes how this can be fostered at the interpersonal relationship level.

The Military Theorists

In the 1980s some business strategists realized that there was a vast knowledge base stretching back thousands of years that they had barely examined. They turned to military strategy for guidance. Military strategy books such as The Art of War by Sun Tzu, On War by von Clausewitz, and The Red Book by Mao Tse Tung became instant business classics. From Sun Tzu they learned the tactical side of military strategy and specific tactical prescriptions. From Von Clausewitz they learned the dynamic and unpredictable nature of military strategy. From Mao Tse Tung they learned the principles of guerrilla warfare. The main marketing warfare books were:

- Business War Games by Barrie James, 1984
- Marketing Warfare by Al Ries and Jack Trout, 1986
- Leadership Secrets of Attila the Hun by Wess Roberts, 1987

Philip Kotler was a well-known proponent of marketing warfare strategy. There were generally thought to be four types of business warfare theories. They are:

- Offensive marketing warfare strategies
- Defensive marketing warfare strategies
- Flanking marketing warfare strategies
- Guerrilla marketing warfare strategies

The marketing warfare literature also examined leadership and motivation, intelligence gathering, types of marketing weapons, logistics, and communications.

By the turn of the century marketing warfare strategies had gone out of favour. It was felt that they were limiting. There were many situations in which non-confrontational approaches were more appropriate. The "Strategy of the Dolphin" was developed in the mid 1990s to give guidance as to when to use aggressive strategies and when to use passive strategies. A variety of aggressiveness strategies were developed.

In 1993, J. Moore used a similar metaphor. Instead of using military terms, he created an ecological theory of predators and prey (see ecological model of competition), a sort of Darwinian management strategy in which market interactions mimic long term ecological stability.

Strategic Change

In 1970, Alvin Toffler in Future Shockdescribed a trend towards accelerating rates of change. He illustrated how social and technological norms had shorter lifespans with each generation, and he questioned society's ability to cope with the resulting turmoil and anxiety. In past generations periods of change were always punctuated with times of stability. This allowed society to assimilate the change and deal with it before the next change arrived. But these periods of stability are getting shorter and by the late 20th century had all but disappeared. In 1980 in The Third Wave, Toffler characterized this shift to relentless change as the defining feature of the third phase of civilization (the first two phases being the agricultural and industrial waves). He claimed that the dawn of this new phase will cause great anxiety for those that grew up in the previous phases, and will cause much conflict and opportunity in the business world. Hundreds of authors, particularly since the early 1990s, have attempted to explain what this means for business strategy.

In 1997, Watts Waker and Jim Taylor called this upheaval a "500 year delta." They claimed these major upheavals occur every 5 centuries. They said we are currently making the transition from the "Age of Reason" to a new chaotic Age of Access. Jeremy Rifkin (2000) popularized and expanded this term, "age of access" three years later in his book of the same name.

In 1968, Peter Drucker (1969) coined the phrase Age of Discontinuity to describe the way change forces disruptions into the continuity of our lives. In an age of continuity attempts to predict the future by extrapolating from the past can be somewhat accurate. But according to Drucker, we are now in an age of discontinuity and extrapolating from the past is hopelessly ineffective. We cannot assume that trends that exist today will continue into the future. He identifies four sources of discontinuity: new technologies, globalization, cultural pluralism, and knowledge capital.

In 2000, Gary Hamel discussed strategic decay, the notion that the value of all strategies, no matter how brilliant, decays over time.

In 1978, Dereck Abell (Abell, D. 1978) described strategic windows and stressed the importance of the timing (both entrance and exit) of any given strategy. This has led some strategic planners to build planned obsolescence into their strategies.

In 1989, Charles Handy identified two types of change. Strategic drift is a gradual change that occurs so subtly that it is not noticed until it is too late. By contrast, transformational change is sudden and radical. It is typically caused by discontinuities (or exogenous shocks) in the business environment. The point where a new trend is initiated is called a strategic inflection point by Andy Grove. Inflection points can be subtle or radical.

In 2000, Malcolm Gladwell discussed the importance of the tipping point, that point where a trend or fad acquires critical mass and takes off.

In 1983, Noel Tichy recognized that because we are all beings of habit we tend to repeat what we are comfortable with. He wrote that this is a trap that constrains our creativity, prevents us from exploring new ideas, and hampers our dealing with the full complexity of new issues. He developed a systematic method of dealing with change that involved looking at any new issue from three angles:

technical and production, political and resource allocation, and corporate culture.

In 1990, Richard Pascale (Pascale, R. 1990) wrote that relentless change requires that businesses continuously reinvent themselves. His famous maxim is "Nothing fails like success" by which he means that what was a strength yesterday becomes the root of weakness today, We tend to depend on what worked yesterday and refuse to let go of what worked so well for us in the past. Prevailing strategies become self-confirming. In order to avoid this trap, businesses must stimulate a spirit of inquiry and healthy debate. They must encourage a creative process of self renewal based on constructive conflict.

In 1996, Art Kleiner (1996) claimed that to foster a corporate culture that embraces change, you have to hire the right people; heretics, heroes, outlaws, and visionaries. The conservative bureaucrat that made such a good middle manager in yesterday's hierarchical organizations is of little use today. A decade earlier Peters and Austin (1985) had stressed the importance of nurturing champions and heroes. They said we have a tendency to dismiss new ideas, so to overcome this, we should support those few people in the organization that have the courage to put their career and reputation on the line for an unproven idea.

In 1996, Adrian Slywotsky showed how changes in the business environment are reflected in value migrations between industries, between companies, and within companies. He claimed that recognizing the patterns behind these value migrations is necessary if we wish to understand the world of chaotic change. In "Profit Patterns" (1999) he described businesses as being in a state of strategic anticipation as they try to spot emerging patterns. Slywotsky and his team identified 30 patterns that have transformed industry after industry.

In 1997, Clayton Christensen (1997) took the position that great companies can fail precisely because they do everything right since the capabilities of the organization also defines its disabilities. Christensen's thesis is that outstanding companies lose their market leadership when confronted with disruptive technology. He called the approach to discovering the emerging markets for disruptive technologies agnostic marketing, i.e., marketing under the implicit assumption that no one-not the company, not the customers-can know how or in what quantities a disruptive product can or will be used before they have experience using it.

A number of strategists use scenario planning techniques to deal with change. Kees van der Heijden (1996), for example, says that change and uncertainty make "optimum strategy" determination impossible. We have neither the time nor the information required for such a calculation. The best we can hope for is what he calls "the most skillful process". The way Peter Schwartz put it in 1991 is that strategic outcomes cannot be known in advance so the sources of competitive advantage cannot be predetermined. The fast changing business environment is too uncertain for us to find sustainable value in formulas of excellence or competitive advantage. Instead, scenario planning is a technique in which multiple outcomes can be developed, their implications assessed, and their likeliness of occurrence evaluated. According to Pierre Wack, scenario planning is about insight, complexity, and subtlety, not about formal analysis and numbers.

In 1988, Henry Mintzberg looked at the changing world around him and decided it was time to reexamine how strategic management was done. He examined the strategic process and concluded it was much more fluid and unpredictable than people had thought. Because of this, he could not point to one process that could be called strategic planning. Instead he concludes that there are five types of strategies. They are:

- Strategy as plan-a direction, guide, course of action-intention rather than actual
- Strategy as ploy-a maneuver intended to outwit a competitor
- Strategy as pattern-a consistent pattern of past behaviour-realized rather than intended
- Strategy as position-locating of brands, products, or companies within the conceptual framework of consumers or other stakeholders-strategy determined primarily by factors outside the firm
- Strategy as perspective-strategy determined primarily by a master strategist

In 1998, Mintzberg developed these five types of management strategy into 10 "schools of thought". These 10 schools are grouped into three categories. The first group is prescriptive or normative. It consists of the informal design and conception school, the formal planning school, and the analytical positioning school. The second group, consisting of six schools, is more concerned with how strategic management is actually done, rather than prescribing optimal plans or positions. The six schools are the entrepreneurial, visionary, or great leader school, the cognitive or mental process school, the learning, adaptive, or emergent process school, the power or negotiation school, the corporate culture or collective process school, and the business environment or reactive school. The third and final group consists of one school, the configuration or transformation school, an hybrid of the other schools organized into stages, organizational life cycles, or "episodes".

In 1999, Constantinos Markides also wanted to reexamine the nature of strategic planning itself. He describes strategy formation and implementation as an on-going, never-ending, integrated process requiring continuous reassessment and reformation. Strategic management is planned and emergent, dynamic, and interactive. J. Moncrieff (1999) also stresses strategy dynamics. He recognized that strategy is partially deliberate and partially unplanned. The unplanned element comes from two sources: emergent strategies (result from the emergence of opportunities and threats in the environment) and Strategies in action (ad hoc actions by many people from all parts of the organization).

Some business planners are starting to use a complexity theory approach to strategy. Complexity can be thought of as chaos with a dash of order. Chaos theory deals with turbulent systems that rapidly become disordered. Complexity is not quite so unpredictable. It involves multiple agents interacting in such a way that a glimpse of structure may appear. Axelrod, R., Holland, J., and Kelly, S. and Allison, M.A., call these systems of multiple actions and .ctions complex adaptive systems. Axelrod asserts that ,ather than fear complexity, business should harness it. He says this can best be done when "there are many participants, numerous interactions, much trial and error learning, and abundant attempts to imitate each others' successes". In 2000, E. Dudik wrote that an organization must develop a mechanism for understanding the source and level of complexity it will face in the future and then transform itself into a complex adaptive system in order to deal with it.

Information and Technology Driven Strategy

Peter Drucker had theorized the rise of the "knowledge worker" back in the 1950s. He described how fewer workers would be doing physical labour, and more would be applying their minds. In 1984, John Nesbitt theorized that the future would be driven largely by information: companies that managed information well could obtain an advantage, however the profitability of what he calls the "information float" (information that the company had and others desired) would all but disappear as inexpensive computers made information more accessible.

Daniel Bell (1985) examined the sociological consequences of information technology, while Gloria Schuck and Shoshana Zuboff looked at psychological factors. Zuboff, in her five year study of eight pioneering corporations made the important distinction between "automating technologies" and "infomating technologies". She studied the effect that both had on individual workers, managers, and organizational structures. She largely confirmed Peter Drucker's predictions three decades earlier, about the importance of flexible decentralized structure, work teams, knowledge sharing, and the central role of the knowledge worker. Zuboff also detected a new basis for managerial authority, based not on position or hierarchy, but on knowledge (also predicted by Drucker) which she called "participative management".

In 1990, Peter Senge, who had collaborated with Arie de Geus at Dutch Shell, borrowed de Geus' notion of the learning organization, expanded it, and popularized it. The underlying theory is that a company's ability to gather, analyze, and use information is a necessary requirement for business success in the information age. (See organizational learning.) In order to do this, Senge claimed that an organization would need to be structured such that:

- People can continuously expand their capacity to learn and be productive,
- New patterns of thinking are nurtured,
- Collective aspirations are encouraged, and
- People are encouraged to see the "whole picture" together.

Senge identified five components of a learning organization. They are:

- Personal responsibility, self reliance, and mastery-We accept that we are the masters of our own destiny. We make decisions and live with the consequences of them. When a problem needs to be fixed, or an opportunity exploited, we take the initiative to learn the required skills to get it done.
- Mental models-We need to explore our personal mental models to understand the subtle effect they have on our behaviour.
- Shared vision-The vision of where we want to be in the future is discussed and communicated to all. It provides guidance and energy for the journey ahead.
- Team learning-We learn together in teams. This involves a shift from "a spirit of advocacy to a spirit of enquiry".
- Systems thinking-We look at the whole rather than the parts. This is what Senge calls the "Fifth discipline". It is the glue that integrates the other four into a coherent strategy. For an alternative approach to the "learning organization", see Garratt, B. (1987).

Since 1990 many theorists have written on the strategic importance of information, including J.B. Quinn, J. Carlos Jarillo, D.L. Barton, Manuel Castells, J.P. Lieleskin, Thomas Stewart, K.E. Sveiby, Gilbert J. Probst, and Shapiro and Varian to name just a few.

Thomas A. Stewart, for example, uses the term intellectual capital to describe the investment an organization makes in knowledge. It is comprised of human capital (the knowledge inside the heads of employees), customer capital (the knowledge inside the heads of customers that decide to buy from you), and structural capital (the knowledge that resides in the company itself).

Manuel Castells, describes a network society characterized by: globalization, organizations structured as a network, instability of employment, and a social divide between those with access to information technology and those without.

Stan Davis and Christopher Meyer (1998) have combined three variables to define what they call the BLUR equation. The speed of change, Internet connectivity, and intangible knowledge value, when multiplied together yields a society's rate of BLUR. The three variables interact and reinforce each other making this relationship highly non-linear.

Regis McKenna posits that life in the high tech information age is what he called a "real time experience". Events occur in real time. To ever more demanding customers "now" is what matters. Pricing will more and more become variable pricing changing with each transaction, often exhibiting first degree price discrimination. Customers expect immediate service, customized to their needs, and will be prepared to pay a premium price for it. He claimed that the new basis for competition will be time based competition.

Geoffrey Moore (1991) and R. Frank and P. Cook also detected a shift in the nature of competition. In industries with high technology content, technical standards become established and this gives the dominant firm a near monopoly. The same is true of networked industries in which interoperability requires compatibility between users. An example is word processor documents. Once a product has gained market dominance, other products, even far superior products, cannot compete. Moore showed how firms could attain this enviable position by using E.M. Rogers five stage adoption process and focusing on one group of customers at a time, using each group as a base for marketing to the next group. The most difficult step is making the transition between visionaries and pragmatists (See Crossing the Chasm). If successful a firm can create a bandwagon effect in which the momentum builds and your product becomes a de facto standard.

Evans and Wurster describe how industries with a high information component are being transformed. They cite Encarta's demolition of the Encyclopedia Britannica (whose sales have plummeted 80% since their peak of $650 million in 1990). Many speculate that Encarta's reign will be short-lived, eclipsed by collaborative encyclopedias like Wikipedia that can operate at very low marginal costs. Evans also mentions the music industry which is desperately looking for a new business model. The upstart information savvy firms, unburdened by cumbersome physical assets, are changing the competitive landscape, redefining market segments, and disintermediating some channels. One manifestation of this is personalized marketing. Information technology allows marketers to treat each individual as its own market, a market of one. Traditional ideas of market segments will no longer be relevant if personalized marketing is successful.

The technology sector has provided some strategies directly. For example, from the software development industry agile software development provides a model for shared development processes.

Access to information systems have allowed senior managers to take a much more comprehensive view of strategic management than ever before. The most notable of the comprehensive systems is the balanced scorecard approach developed in the early 1990's by Drs. Robert S. Kaplan (Harvard Business School) and David Norton (Kaplan, R. and Norton, D. 1992). It measures several factors financial, marketing, production, organizational development, and new product development in order to achieve a 'balanced' perspective.

The Psychology of Strategic Management

Several psychologists have conducted studies to determine the psychological patterns involved in strategic management. Typically senior managers have been asked how they go about making strategic decisions. A 1938 treatise by Chester Barnard, that was based on his own experience as a business executive, sees the process as informal, intuitive, non-routinized, and involving primarily oral, 2-way communications. Bernard says "The process is the sensing of the organization as a whole and the total situation relevant to it. It transcends the capacity of merely intellectual methods, and the techniques of discriminating the factors of the situation. The terms pertinent to it are "feeling", "judgement", "sense", "proportion", "balance", "appropriateness". It is a matter of art rather than science."

In 1973, Henry Mintzberg found that senior managers typically deal with unpredictable situations so they strategize in ad hoc, flexible, dynamic, and implicit ways. He says, "The job breeds adaptive information-manipulators who prefer the live concrete situation. The manager works in an environment of stimulous-response, and he develops in his work a clear preference for live action."

In 1982, John Kotter studied the daily activities of 15 executives and concluded that they spent most of their time developing and working a network of relationships from which they gained general insights and specific details to be used in making strategic decisions. They tended to use "mental road maps" rather than systematic planning techniques. Daniel Isenberg's 1984 study of senior managers found that their decisions were highly intuitive. Executives often sensed what they were going to do before they could explain why. He claimed in 1986 that one of the reasons for this is the complexity of strategic decisions and the resultant information uncertainty.

Shoshana Zuboff (1988) claims that information technology is widening the divide between senior managers (who typically make strategic decisions) and operational level managers (who typically make routine decisions). She claims that prior to the widespread use of computer systems, managers, even at the most senior level, engaged in both strategic decisions and routine administration, but as computers facilitated (She called it "deskilled") routine processes, these activities were moved further down the hierarchy, leaving senior management free for strategic decions making. In 1977, Abraham Zaleznik identified a difference between leaders and managers. He describes leadershipleaders as visionaries who inspire. They care about substance. Whereas managers are claimed to care about process, plans, and form. He also claimed in 1989 that the rise of the manager was the main factor that caused the decline of American business in the 1970s and 80s. Lack of leadership is most damaging at the level of strategic management where it can paralyze an entire organization.

According to Corner, Kinichi, and Keats, strategic decision making in organizations occurs at two levels: individual and aggregate. They have developed a model of parallel strategic decision making. The model identifies two parallel processes both of which involve getting attention, encoding information, storage and retrieval of information, strategic choice, strategic outcome, and feedback. The individual and organizational processes are not independent however. They interact at each stage of the process.

Reasons why Strategic Plans Fail

There are many reasons why strategic plans fail, especially:

- Failure to understand the customer
  - Why do they buy
  - Is there a real need for the product
  - inadequate or incorrect marketing research
- Inability to predict environmental reaction
  - What will competitors do
- Fighting brands
- Price wars
  - Will government intervene
- Over-estimation of resource competence
  - Can the staff, equipment, and processes handle the new strategy
  - Failure to develop new employee and management skills
- Failure to coordinate
  - Reporting and control relationships not adequate
  - Organizational structure not flexible enough
- Failure to obtain senior management commitment
  - Failure to get management involved right from the start
  - Failure to obtain sufficient company resources to accomplish task
- Failure to obtain employee commitment
  - New strategy not well explained to employees
  - No incentives given to workers to embrace the new strategy
- Under-estimation of time requirements
  - No critical path analysis done

- Failure to follow the plan
  - No follow through after initial planning
  - No tracking of progress against plan
  - No consequences for above
- Failure to manage change
  - Inadequate understanding of the internal resistance to change
  - Lack of vision on the relationships between processes, technology and organization
- Poor communications
  - Insufficient information sharing among stakeholders
  - Exclusion of stakeholders and delegates

CRITICISMS OF STRATEGIC MANAGEMENT

Although a sense of direction is important, it can also stifle creativity, especially if it is rigidly enforced. In an uncertain and ambiguous world, fluidity can be more important than a finely tuned strategic compass. When a strategy becomes internalized into a corporate culture, it can lead to group think. It can also cause an organization to define itself too narrowly. An example of this is marketing myopia.

Many theories of strategic management tend to undergo only brief periods of popularity. A summary of these theories thus inevitably exhibits survivorship bias (itself an area of research in strategic management). Many theories tend either to be too narrow in focus to build a complete corporate strategy on, or too general and abstract to be applicable to specific situations. Populism or faddishness can have an impact on a particular theory's life cycle and may see application in inappropriate circumstances. See business philosophies and popular management theories for a more critical view of management theories.

In 2000, Gary Hamel coined the term strategic convergence to explain the limited scope of the strategies being used by rivals in greatly differing circumstances. He lamented that strategies converge more than they should, because the more successful ones get imitated by firms that do not understand that the strategic process involves designing a custom strategy for the specifics of each situation.

Ram Charan, aligning with a popular marketing tagline, believes that strategic planning must not dominate action. "Just do it!", while not quite what he meant, is a phrase that nevertheless comes to mind when combatting analysis paralysis.

Journals Devoted Primarily to Strategic Management

- Strategic Management Journal
- Harvard Business Review
- The Journal of Business Strategy
- Long Range Planning-house journal of the Strategic Planning Society
- Strategy and Leadership

2

MARKETING MANAGEMENT

Marketing management is a business discipline focused on the practical application of marketing techniques and the management of a firm's marketing resources and activities. Marketing managers are often responsible for influencing the level, timing, and composition of customer demand in a manner that will achieve the company's objectives.

DEFINITION AND SCOPE

There is no universally accepted definition of the term. In part, this is due to the fact that the role of a marketing manager can vary significantly based on a business' size, corporate culture, and industry context. For example, in a large consumer products company, the marketing manager may act as the overall general manager of his or her assigned product category or brand with full profit & loss responsibility. In contrast, a small law firm may have no marketing personnel at all, requiring the firm's partners to make marketing management decisions on a largely ad-hoc basis.

Vispy Doctor of Ormax (www.ormaxworld.com), India's leading marketing strategy expert, defines marketing management as applying available resources to create or change the perception of a product or service in the eyes of its target audience by the application of research and communication media.

In the widely used text Marketing Management (2006), Philip Kotler and Kevin Lane Keller define marketing management as "the art and science of choosing target markets and getting, keeping and growing customers through creating, delivering, and communicating superior customer value."

From this perspective, the scope of marketing management is quite broad. The implication of such a definition is that any activity or resource the firm uses to acquire customers and manage the company's relationships with them is within the purview of marketing management. Additionally, the Kotler and Keller definition encompasses both the development of new products and services and their delivery to customers.

Noted marketing expert Regis McKenna expressed a similar viewpoint in his influential 1991 Harvard Business Review article "Marketing is Everything." McKenna argued that because marketing management encompasses all factors that influence a company's ability to deliver value to customers, it must be "all-pervasive, part of everyone's job description, from the receptionists to the Board of Directors."

This view is also consistent with the perspective of management guru Peter Drucker, who wrote: "Because the purpose of business is to create a customer, the business enterprise has two--and only these two--basic functions: marketing and innovation. Marketing and innovation produce results; all the rest are costs. Marketing is the distinguishing, unique function of the business."

But because many businesses operate with a much more limited definition of marketing, such statements can appear controversial, or even ludicrous to some business executives. This is especially true in those companies where the marketing department is responsible for little more than developing sales brochures and executing advertising campaigns.

The broader, more sophisticated definitions of marketing management from Drucker, Kotler and other scholars are therefore juxtaposed against the narrower operating reality of many businesses. The source of confusion here is often that inside any given firm, the term marketing management may be interpreted to mean whatever the marketing department happens to do, rather than a term that encompasses all marketing activities--even those marketing activities that are actually performed by other departments, such as the sales, finance, or operations departments. If, for example, the finance department of a given company makes pricing decisions (for deals, proposals, contracts, etc.), that finance department has responsibility for an important component of marketing management--pricing.

ACTIVITIES AND FUNCTIONS

Marketing management therefore encompasses a wide variety of functions and activities, although the marketing department itself may be responsible for only a subset of these. Regardless of the organizational unit of the firm responsible for managing them, marketing management functions and activities include the following:

MARKETING RESEARCH AND ANALYSIS

In order to make fact-based decisions regarding marketing strategy and design effective, cost-efficient implementation programs, firms must possess a detailed, objective understanding of their own business and the market in which they operate. In analyzing these issues, the discipline of marketing management often overlaps with the related discipline of strategic planning.

Traditionally, marketing analysis was structured into three areas: Customer analysis, Company analysis, and Competitor analysis (so-called "3Cs" analysis). More recently, it has become fashionable in some marketing circles to divide these further into certain five "Cs": Customer analysis, Company analysis, Collaborator analysis, Competitor analysis, and analysis of the industry Context.

The focus of customer analysis is to develop a scheme for market segmentation, breaking down the market into various constituent groups of customers, which are called customer segments or market segments. Marketing managers work to develop detailed profiles of each segment, focusing on any number of variables that may differ among the segments: demographic, psychographic, geographic, behavioral, needs-benefit, and other factors may all be examined. Marketers also attempt to track these segments' perceptions of the various products in the market using tools such as perceptual mapping.

In company analysis, marketers focus on understanding the company's cost structure and cost position relative to competitors, as well as working to identify a firm's core competencies and other competitively distinct company resources. Marketing managers may also work with the accounting department to analyze the profits the firm is generating from various product lines and customer accounts. The company may also conduct periodic brand audits to assess the strength of its brands and sources of brand equity.

The firm's collaborators may also be profiled, which may include various suppliers, distributors and other channel partners, joint venture partners, and others. An analysis of complementary products may also be performed if such products exist. Marketing management employs various tools from economics and competitive strategy to analyze the industry context in which the firm operates. These include Porter's five forces, analysis of strategic groups of competitors, value chain analysis and others. Depending on the industry, the regulatory context may also be important to examine in detail.

In Competitor analysis, marketers build detailed profiles of each competitor in the market, focusing especially on their relative competitive strengths and weaknesses using SWOT analysis. Marketing managers will examine each competitor's cost structure, sources of profits, resources and competencies, competitive positioning and product differentiation, degree of vertical integration, historical responses to industry developments, and other factors. Marketing management often finds it necessary to invest in research to collect the data required to perform accurate marketing analysis. As such, they often conduct market research (alternately marketing research) to obtain this information. Marketers employ a variety of techniques to conduct market research, but some of the more common include:

- Qualitative marketing research, such as focus groups
- Quantitative marketing research, such as statistical surveys
- Experimental techniques such as test markets
- Observational techniques such as ethnographic (on-site) observation

Marketing managers may also design and oversee various environmental scanning and competitive intelligence processes to help identify trends and inform the company's marketing analysis.

MARKETING STRATEGY

Once the company has obtained an adequate understanding of the customer base and its own competitive position in the industry, marketing managers are able to make key strategic decisions and develop a marketing strategy designed to maximize the revenues and profits of the firm. The selected strategy may aim for any of a variety of specific objectives, including optimizing short-term unit margins, revenue growth, market share, long-term profitability, or other goals.

To achieve the desired objectives, marketers typically identify one or more target customer segments which they intend to pursue. Customer segments are often selected as targets because they score highly on two dimensions:

(1) The segment is attractive to serve because it is large, growing, makes frequent purchases, is not price sensitive (i.e. is willing to pay high prices), or other factors; and

(2) The company has the resources and capabilities to compete for the segment's business, can meet their needs better than the competition, and can do so profitably. In fact, a commonly cited definition of marketing is simply "meeting needs profitably."

The implication of selecting target segments is that the business will subsequently allocate more resources to acquire and retain customers in the target segment(s) than it will for other, non-targeted customers. In some cases, the firm may go so far as to turn away customers that are not in its target segment. The doorman at a swanky nightclub, for example, may deny entry to unfashionably dressed individuals because the business has made a strategic decision to target the "high fashion" segment of nightclub patrons.

In conjunction with targeting decisions, marketing managers will identify the desired positioning they want the company, product, or brand to occupy in the target customer's mind. This positioning is often an encapsulation of a key benefit the company's product or service offers that is differentiated and superior to the benefits offered by competitive products. For example, Volvo has traditionally positioned its products in the automobile market in North America in order to be perceived as the leader in "safety", whereas BMW has traditionally positioned its brand to be perceived as the leader in "performance."

Ideally, a firm's positioning can be maintained over a long period of time because the company possesses, or can develop, some form of sustainable competitive advantage. The positioning should also be sufficiently relevant to the target segment such that it will drive the purchasing behavior of target customers.

IMPLEMENTATION PLANNING

After the firm's strategic objectives have been identified, the target market selected, and the desired positioning for the company, product or brand has been determined, marketing managers focus on how to best implement the chosen strategy. Traditionally, this has involved implementation planning across the "4Ps" of marketing: Product management, Pricing, Place (i.e. sales and distribution channels), and Promotion.

Taken together, the company's implementation choices across the 4Ps are often described as the marketing mix, meaning the mix of elements the business will employ to "go to market" and execute the marketing strategy. The overall goal for the marketing mix is to consistently deliver a compelling value proposition that reinforces the firm's chosen positioning, builds customer loyalty and brand equity among target customers, and achieves the firm's marketing and financial objectives.

In many cases, marketing management will develop a marketing plan to specify how the company will execute the chosen strategy and achieve the business' objectives. The content of marketing plans varies from firm to firm, but commonly includes:

- An executive summary
- Situation analysis to summarize facts and insights gained from market research and marketing analysis
- The company's mission statement or long-term strategic vision
- A statement of the company's key objectives, often subdivided into marketing objectives and financial objectives
- The marketing strategy the business has chosen, specifying the target segments to be pursued and the competitive positioning to be achieved
- Implementation choices for each element of the marketing mix (the 4Ps)
- A summary of required investments (in people, programs, IT systems, etc.)
- Financial analysis, projections and forecasted results
- A timeline or high-level project plan
- Metrics, measurements and control processes
- A list of key risks and strategies for managing these risks

PROJECT, PROCESS, AND VENDOR MANAGEMENT

Once the key implementation initiatives have been identified, marketing managers work to oversee the execution of the marketing plan. Marketing executives may therefore manage any number of specific projects, such as sales force management initiatives, product development efforts, channel marketing programs and the execution of public relations and advertising campaigns. Marketers use a variety of project management techniques to ensure projects achieve their objectives while keeping to established schedules and budgets.

More broadly, marketing managers work to design and improve the effectiveness of core marketing processes, such as new product development, brand management, marketing communications, and pricing. Marketers may employ the tools of business process reengineering to ensure these processes are properly designed, and use a variety of process management techniques to keep them operating smoothly.

Effective execution may require management of both internal resources and a variety of external vendors and service providers, such as the firm's advertising agency. Marketers may therefore coordinate with the company's Purchasing department on the procurement of these services. from divya dutt

ORGANIZATIONAL MANAGEMENT AND LEADERSHIP

Marketing management usually requires leadership of a department or group of professionals engaged in marketing activities. Often, this oversight will extend beyond the company's marketing department itself, requiring the marketing manager to provide cross-functional leadership for various marketing activities. This may require extensive interaction with the human resources department on issues such as recruiting, training, leadership development, performance appraisals, compensation, and other topics.

Marketing management may spend a fair amount of time building or maintaining a marketing orientation for the business. Achieving a market orientation, also known as "customer focus" or the "marketing concept", requires building consensus at the senior management level and then driving customer focus down into the organization.

Cultural barriers may exist in a given business unit or functional area that the marketing manager must address in order to achieve this goal. Additionally, marketing executives often act as a "brand champion" and work to enforce corporate identity standards across the enterprise.

In larger organizations, especially those with multiple business units, top marketing managers may need to coordinate across several marketing departments and also resources from finance, R&D, engineering, operations, manufacturing, or other functional areas to implement the marketing plan. In order to effectively manage these resources, marketing executives may need to spend much of their time focused on political issues and inter-departmental negotiations.

The effectiveness of a marketing manager may therefore depend on his or her ability to make the internal "sale" of various marketing programs equally as much as the external customer's reaction to such programs.

REPORTING, MEASUREMENT, FEEDBACK AND CONTROL SYSTEMS

Marketing management employs a variety of metrics to measure progress against objectives. It is the responsibility of marketing managers--in the marketing department or elsewhere--to ensure that the execution of marketing programs achieves the desired objectives and does so in a cost-efficient manner.

Marketing management therefore often makes use of various organizational control systems, such as sales forecasts, sales force and reseller incentive programs, sales force management systems, and customer relationship management tools (CRM). Recently, some software vendors have begun using the term "marketing operations management" or "marketing resource management" to describe systems that facilitate an integrated approach for controlling marketing resources. In some cases, these efforts may be linked to various supply chain management systems, such as enterprise resource planning (ERP), material requirements planning (MRP), efficient consumer response (ECR), and inventory management systems.

Measuring the return on investment (ROI) of and marketing effectiveness various marketing initiatives is a significant problem for marketing management. Various market research, accounting and financial tools are used to help estimate the ROI of marketing investments. Brand valuation, for example, attempts to identify the percentage of a company's market value that is generated by the company's brands, and thereby estimate the financial value of specific investments in brand equity. Another technique, integrated marketing communications (IMC), is a CRM database-driven approach that attempts to estimate the value of marketing mix executions based on the changes in customer behavior these executions generate.

FINANCE

Finance studies and addresses the ways in which individuals, businesses, and organizations raise, allocate, and use monetary resources over time, taking into account the risks entailed in their projects. The term "finance" may thus incorporate any of the following:

- The study of money and other assets;
- The management and control of those assets;
- Profiling and managing project risks;
- The science of managing money;
- As a verb, "to finance" is to provide funds for business or for an individual's large purchases (car, home, etc.).

The activity of finance is the application of a set of techniques that individuals and organizations (entities) use to manage their money, particularly the differences between income and expenditure and the risks of their investments.

An income that exceeds its expenditure can lend or invest the excess income. On the other hand, an entity whose income is less than its expenditure can raise capital by borrowing or selling equity claims, decreasing its expenses, or increasing its income. The lender can find a borrower, a financial intermediary, such as a bank or buy notes or bonds in the bond market. The lender receives interest, the borrower pays a higher interest than the lender receives, and the financial intermediary pockets the difference. A bank aggregates the activities of many borrowers and lenders. A bank accepts deposits from lenders, on which it pays the interest. The bank then lends these deposits to borrowers. Banks allow borrowers and lenders, of different sizes, to coordinate their activity. Banks are thus compensators of money flows in space.

A specific example of corporate finance is the sale of stock by a company to institutional investors like investment banks, who in turn generally sell it to the public. The stock gives whoever owns it part ownership in that company. If you buy one share of XYZ Inc, and they have 100 shares outstanding (held by investors), you are 1/100 owner of that company. Of course, in return for the stock, the company receives cash, which it uses to expand its business in a process called "equity financing". Equity financing mixed with the sale of bonds (or any other debt financing) is called the company's capital structure.

Finance is used by individuals (personal finance), by governments (public finance), by businesses (corporate finance), as well as by a wide variety of organizations including schools and non-profit organizations. In general, the goals of each of the above activities are achieved through the use of appropriate financial instruments, with consideration to their institutional setting. Finance is one of the most important aspects of business management. Without proper financial planning a new enterprise is unlikely to be successful. Managing money (a liquid asset) is essential to ensure a secure future, both for the individual and an organization.

Personal Finance

Questions in personal finance revolve around

- How much money will be needed by an individual (or by a family) at various points in the future?
- Where will this money come from (e.g. savings or borrowing)?
- How can people protect themselves against unforeseen events in their lives, and risk in financial markets?
- How can family assets be best transferred across generations (bequests and inheritance)?
- How do taxes (tax subsidies or penalties) affect personal financial decisions?

Personal financial decisions may involve paying for education, financing durable goods such as real estate and cars, buying insurance, e.g. health and property insurance, investing and saving for retirement. Personal financial decisions may also involve paying for a loan.

Corporate Finance

Managerial or corporate finance is the task of providing the funds for a corporation's activities. For small business, this is referred to as SME finance. It generally involves balancing risk and profitability, while attempting to maximize an entity's wealth and the value of its stock. Long term funds are provided by ownership equity and long-term credit, often in the form of bonds. The balance between these forms the company's capital structure. Short-term funding or working capital is mostly provided by banks extending a line of credit. On the bond market, borrowers package their debt in the form of bonds. The borrower receives the money that it borrows by selling the bond, which includes a promise to repay the value of the bond with interest. The purchaser of a bond can resell it so that the actual recipient of the interest payments can change over time. Bonds allow lenders to recoup the value of their loan by simply selling the bond.

Another business decision concerning finance is investment, or fund management. An investment is an acquisition of an asset in the hope that it will maintain or increase its value. In investment management--in choosing a portfolio--one has to decide what, how much and when to invest. To do this, a company must:

- Identify relevant objectives and constraints: institution or individual goals, time horizon, risk aversion and tax considerations;
- Identify the appropriate strategy: active v. passive--hedging strategy
- Measure the portfolio performance

Financial management is duplicate with the financial function of the Accounting profession. However, financial accounting is more concerned with the reporting of historical financial information, while the financial decision is directed toward the future of the firm.

Capital

Capital is the money which gives the business the power to buy goods to be used in the production of other goods or the offering of a service.

Sources of Capital

Capital Market

- Long-term funds are bought and sold:
  - Shares
  - Debentures
  - Long-term loans, often with a mortgage bond as security
  - Reserve funds
  - Euro Bonds

Money Market

- Financial institutions can use short-term savings to lend out in the form of short-term loans:
  - Credit on open account
  - Bank overdraft
  - Short-term loans
  - Bills of exchange
  - Factoring of debtors

Borrowed Capital

This is capital which the business borrows from institutions or people, and includes debentures:

- Redeemable debentures
- Irredeemable debentures
- Debentures to bearer
- Hardcore debentures

Own Capital

This is capital that owners of a business (shareholders and partners, for example) provide:

- Preference shares:
  - — Ordinary preference shares
  - — Cumulative preference shares
  - — Participating preference shares
- Ordinary shares
- Bonus shares
- Founders' shares

Differences between Shares and Debentures

- Shareholders are effectively owners; debenture-holders are creditors.
- Shareholders may vote at AGMs and be elected as directors; debenture-holders may not vote at AGMs or be elected as directors.
- Shareholders receive profit in the form of dividends; debenture-holders receive a fixed rate of interest.
- If there is no profit, the shareholder does not receive a dividend; interest is paid to debenture-holders regardless of whether or not a profit has been made.

Fixed Capital

This is money which is used to purchase assets that will remain permanently in the business and help it to make a profit.

Factors Determining Fixed Capital Requirements

- Nature of business
- Size of business
- Stage of development
- Capital invested by the owners

Working Capital

This is money which is used to buy stock, pay expenses and finance credit.

Factors Determining Working Capital Requirements

- Size of business
- Stage of development
- Time of production
- Rate of stock turnover
- Buying and selling terms
- Seasonal consumption
- Seasonal production

The Desirability of Budgeting

Capital Budget

This concerns fixed asset requirements for the next five years and how these will be financed.

Cash Budget

Working capital requirements of a business should be monitored at all times to ensure that there are sufficient funds available to meet short-term expenses.

Management of Current Assets

Credit Policy

Credit gives the customer the opportunity to buy goods and services, and pay for them at a later date.

Advantages of Credit Trade

- Usually results in more customers than cash trade
- Can charge more for goods to cover the risk of bad debt

- Gain goodwill and loyalty of customers
- People can buy goods and pay for them at a later date.
- Farmers can buy seeds and implements, and pay for them only after the harvest.
- Stimulates agricultural and industrial production and commerce.

Disadvantages of Credit Trade

- Risk of bad debt
- High administration expenses
- People can buy more than they can afford.
- More working capital needed

Forms of Credit

- Suppliers credit:
  - — Credit on ordinary open account
  - — Instalment sales
  - — Bills of exchange
  - — Credit cards
- Contractor's credit
- Factoring of debtors

Factors which Influence Credit Conditions

- Nature of the business's activities
- Financial position
- Product durability
- Length of production process
- Competition and competitors' credit conditions
- Country's economic position

- Conditions at financial institutions
- Discount for early payment
- Debtor's type of business and financial position

Credit Collection

Overdue Accounts

- Cards arranged alphabetically in card index system
- Attach a notice of overdue account to statement.
- Send a letter asking for settlement of debt.
- Send a second or third letter if first is ineffectual.
- Threaten legal action.

Effective Credit Control

- Increases sales
- Reduces bad debts
- Increases profits
- Builds customer loyalty

Sources of Information on Creditworthiness

- Business references
- Bank references
- Credit agencies
- Chambers of commerce
- Employers
- Credit application forms

Duties of the Credit Department

- Legal action
- Taking necessary steps to ensure settlement of account

- Knowing the credit policy and procedures for credit control
- Setting credit limits
- Ensuring that statements of account are sent out
- Ensuring that thorough checks are carried out on credit customers
- Keeping records of all amounts owing
- Ensuring that debts are settled promptly

Stock

Purpose of Stock Control

- Ensures that enough stock is on hand to satisfy demand.
- Protects and monitors theft.
- Safeguards against having to stockpile.
- Allows for control over selling and cost price.

Stockpiling

This refers to the purchase of stock at the right time, at the right price and in the right quantities.

Advantages

- Losses due to price fluctuations and stock loss kept to a minimum
- Ensures that goods reach customers timeously; better service
- Saves space and storage cost
- Investment of working capital kept to minimum
- No loss in production due to delays

Disadvantages

- Obsolescence

- Danger of fire and theft
- Initial working capital investment is very large
- Losses due to price fluctuation

Influence of Stock Management on Rate of Return

- Right price
- Right quantity
- Right quality
- Right place
- Right time
- Right property

Rate of Stock Turnover

This refers to the number of times per year that the average level of stock is sold. It may be worked out by dividing the cost price of goods sold by the cost price of the average stock level.

Determining Optimum Stock Levels

- Maximum stock level refers to the maximum stock level that may be maintained to ensure cost effectiveness.
- Minimum stock level refers to the point below which the stock level may not go.
- Standard order refers to the amount of stock generally ordered.
- Order level refers to the stock level which calls for an order to be made.

Cash

Reasons for Keeping Cash

- The transaction motive refers to the money kept available to pay expenses.

- The precautionary motive refers to the money kept aside for unforeseen expenses.
- The speculative motive refers the money kept aside to take advantage of suddenly arising opportunities.

Advantages of Sufficient Cash

- Current liabilities may be catered for.
- Cash discounts are given for cash payments.
- Production is kept moving.
- Surplus cash may be invested on a short-term basis.
- The business is able to pay its accounts timeously, allowing for easily-obtained credit.

Management of Fixed Assets

Depreciation

Depreciation is the decrease in the value of an asset due to wear and tear or obsolescence. It is calculated yearly to ensure realistic book values for assets.

Insurance

Insurance is the undertaking of one party to indemnify another, in exchange for a premium, against a certain eventuality.

Uninsurable Risks

- Bad debt
- Changes in fashion
- Time lapses between ordering and delivery
- New machinery or technology
- Different prices at different places

Requirements of an Insurance Contract

- Insurable interest
  - The insured must derive a real financial gain from that which he is insuring, or stand to lose if it is destroyed or lost.
  - The item must belong to the insured.
  - One person may take out insurance on the life of another if the second party owes the first money.
  - Must be some person or item which can, legally, be insured.
  - The insured must have a legal claim to that which he is insuring.
- Good faith
  - Uberrimae fidei refers to absolute honesty and must characterise the dealings of both the insurer and the insured.

Shared Services

There is currently a move towards converging and consolidating Finance provisions into shared services within an organization.

Rather than an organization having a number of separate Finance departments performing the same tasks from different locations a more centralized version can be created.

Finance of States

Country, state, county, city or municipality finance is called public finance. It is concerned with

- Identification of required expenditure of a public sector entity
- Source(s) of that entity's revenue

- The budgeting process
- Debt issuance (municipal bonds) for public works projects

Financial Economics

Financial economics is the branch of economics studying the interrelation of financial variables, such as prices, interest rates and shares, as opposed to those concerning the real economy.

Financial economics concentrates on influences of real economic variables on financial ones, in contrast to pure finance.

It studies:

- Valuation-Determination of the fair value of an asset
  - How risky is the asset? (identification of the asset appropriate discount rate)
  - What cash flows will it produce? (discounting of relevant cash flows)
  - How does the market price compare to similar assets? (relative valuation)
  - Are the cash flows dependent on some other asset or event? (derivatives, contingent claim valuation)
- Financial markets and instruments
  - Commodities-topics
  - Stocks-topics
  - Bonds-topics
  - Money market instruments-topics
  - Derivatives-topics
- Financial institutions and regulation.

Financial Mathematics

Financial mathematics is the main branch of applied mathematics concerned with the financial markets. Financial mathematics is the study of financial data with the tools of mathematics, mainly statistics. Such data can be movements of securities-stocks and bonds etc.-and their relations. Another large subfield is insurance mathematics.

Experimental Finance

Experimental finance aims to establish different market settings and environments to observe experimentally and analyze agents' behavior and the resulting characteristics of trading flows, information diffusion and aggregation, price setting mechanisms, and returns processes. Researchers in experimental finance can study to what extent existing financial economics theory makes valid predictions, and attempt to discover new principles on which such theory can be extended. Research may proceed by conducting trading simulations or by establishing and studying the behaviour of people in artificial competitive market-like settings.

Quantitative behavioral Finance

Quantitative Behavioral Finance is a new discipline that uses mathematical and statistical methodology to understand behavioral biases in conjunction with valuation.

Some of this endeavor has been lead by Gunduz Caginalp (Professor of Mathematics and Editor of Journal of Behavioral Finance during 2001-2004) and collaborators including Vernon Smith (2002 Nobel Laureate in Economics), David Porter, Don Balenovich, Vladimira Ilieva, Ahmet Duran, Huseyin Merdan). Studies by Jeff Madura, Ray Sturm and others have demonstrated significant behavioral effects in stocks and exchange traded funds.

The research can be grouped into the following areas:

1. Empirical studies that demonstrate significant deviations from classical theories.
2. Modeling using the concepts of behavioral effects together with the non-classical assumption of the finiteness of assets.
3. Forecasting based on these methods.
4. Studies of experimental asset markets and use of models to forecast experiments.

3

INFORMATION TECHNOLOGY MANAGEMENT

Information technology management (or IT management) is a combination of two branches of study, information technology and management.

Strictly speaking, there are two incarnations to this definition. One implies the management of a collection of systems, infrastructure, and information that resides on them. Another implies the management of information technologies as a business function.

The first definition stems from the practice of IT Portfolio Management and is the subject of technical manuals and publications of various information technologies providers; while the second definition stems from the discussion and formation of the Information Technology Infrastructure Library (ITIL).

The ITIL has been in practice throughout regions of the world mainly conducted by IT service providers consulting companies. The relative paucity in the use of the best practice set can be attributed to a lack of awareness among IT practitioners. However the lack of ready-to-use tools also presents a significant barrier.

Some organizations that value such practices tend to engage consultants to introduce the practice. Such implementations can conflict with the home-grown culture due to a lack of internal buy-in. Other organizations implement the practices by spending resources to develop in-house tools.

Most in-house developed tools tend to focus on one or a few specific areas where the orgnizations feel the most pains. To reap the full advantages, tools will need to be integrated with the organization's IT data in the center.

MANAGEMENT INFORMATION SYSTEM

Management Information Systems (MIS), sometimes referred to as Information Management and Systems, is the discipline covering the application of people, technologies, and procedures-collectively called information systems-to solving business problems.

Management Information Systems are distinct from regular information systems in that they are used to analyze other information systems applied in operational activities in the organization. Academically, the term is commonly used to refer to the group of information management methods tied to the automation or support of human decision making, e.g. Decision Support Systems, Expert systems, and Executive information systems.

Background

In their infancy, business computers were used for the practical business of computing the payroll and keeping track of accounts payable and receivable. As applications were developed that provided managers with information about sales, inventories, and other data that would help in managing the enterprise, the term "MIS" arose to describe these kinds of applications. Today, the term is used broadly in a number of contexts and includes (but is not limited to): decision support systems, resource and people management applications, project management, and database retrieval applications.

Definition

The terms MIS and information system are often confused. Information systems include systems that are not intended for decision making. MIS is sometimes referred to, in a restrictive sense, as information technology management. That area of study should not be confused with computer science. IT service management is a practitioner-focused discipline. MIS has also some differences with Enterprise Resource Planning (ERP) as ERP incorporates elements that are not necessarily focused on decision support.

Alan Lee defines MIS as "...research in the information systems field examines more than just the technological system, or just the social system, or even the two side by side; in addition, it investigates the phenomena that emerge when the two interact."

IT PORTFOLIO MANAGEMENT

IT portfolio management is the application of systematic management to large classes of items managed by enterprise Information Technology (IT) capabilities. Examples of IT portfolios would be planned initiatives, projects, and ongoing IT services (such as application support). The promise of IT portfolio management is the quantification of previously mysterious IT efforts, enabling measurement and objective evaluation of investment scenarios.

Debates exist on the best way to measure value of IT investment. As pointed out by Jeffery and Leliveld (2004) , companies have spent billions of dollars into IT investment and yet the headlines of mis-spent money are not uncommon. Nicholas Carr (2003) has caused significant controversy in

IT industry and academia by positioning IT as an expense similar to utilities such as electricity.

IT portfolio management started with a project-centric bias, but is evolving to include steady-state portfolio entries such as application maintenance and support, which consume the bulk of IT spending. The challenge for including application maintenance and support in portfolios is that IT budgets tend not to track these efforts at a sufficient level of granularity for effective financial tracking.

The concept is analogous to financial portfolio management, but there are significant differences. IT investments are not liquid, like stocks and bonds (although investment portfolios may also include illiquid assets), and are measured using both financial and non-financial yardsticks (for example, a balanced scorecard approach); a purely financial view is not sufficient.

Financial portfolio assets typically have consistent measurement information (enabling accurate and objective comparisons), and this is at the base of the concept's usefulness in application to IT. However, achieving such universality of measurement is going to take considerable effort in the IT industry.

IT Portfolio management is distinct from IT financial management in that it has an explicitly directive, strategic goal in determining what to continue investing in versus what to divest from.

At its most mature, IT Portfolio management is accomplished through the creation of two portfolios:

- Application Portfolio-Management of this portfolio focuses on the comparing spending against established systems based upon their relative value to the organization. The comparison can be based upon the level of contribution in terms of IT investment's profitability. Additionally, this comparison can also be based upon the non-tangible factors such as organizations' level of experience with a certain technology, users' familiarity with the applications and infrastructure, and external forces such as emergence of new technologies and obsolesce of old ones.

- Project Portfolio-This type of portfolio management specially address the issues with spending on the development of innovative capabilities in terms of potential ROI and reducing investment overlaps in situations where reorganization or acquisition occurs. The management issues with the second type of portfolio management can judged in terms of data cleanliness, maintenance savings, suitability of resulting solution and the relative value of new investments to replace these projects.

Information Technology portfolio management as a systematic discipline is more applicable to larger IT organizations; in smaller organizations its concerns might be generalized into IT planning and governance as a whole.

Benefits of using IT Portfolio Management

Jeffery and Leliveld (2004) have listed several benefits of applying IT portfolio management approach for IT investments. They argue that agility of portfolio management is its biggest advantage over investment approaches and methods. Other benefits include central oversight of budget, risk management, strategic alignment of IT investments, demand and investment management along with standardization of investment procedure, rules and plans.

Implementing IT Portfolio Management

Jeffery and Leliveld (2004) have pointed out a number of hurdles and success factors that CIOs might face while attempting to implement IT portfolio management approach. To overcome these hurdles, simple methods such as proposed by Pisello (2001) can be used.

-Plan-

build retire

Maintain

Other implementation methods include (1) risk profile analysis (figure out what needs to be measured and what risks are associated with it), (2) Decide on the Diversification of projects, infrastructure and technologies (it is an important tool that IT portfolio management provides to judge the level of investments on the basis of how investments should be made in various elements of the portfolio), (3) Continuous Alignment with business goals (highest levels of organizations should have a buy-in in the portfolio) and (4) Continuous Improvement (lessons learned and investment adjustments).

There is no single best way to implement IT portfolio approach and therefore variety of approaches can applied. Obviously the methods are not set on stone and will need altering depending upon the individual circumstances of different organizations.

IT Portfolio Management vs. Balanced Scorecard

The biggest advantage of IT portfolio management is the agility of the investment adjustments. While balanced scorecards also emphasize the use of vision and strategy in any investment decision, oversight and control of operation budgets is not the goal. IT portfolio management allows organizations to adjust the investments based upon the feedback mechanism built into the IT portfolio management.

History

McFarlan is considered to be the first to propose portfolio management approach to IT assets and investments. Further contributions have been made by Weill and Broadbent, , Aitken, Kaplan, and Benson, Bugnitz, and Walton . The ITIL version 2 Business Perspective and Application Management volumes and the ITIL v3 Service Strategy volume also cover it in depth.

Various vendors have offerings explicitly branded as "IT Portfolio Management" solutions.

ISACA's Val IT framework is perhaps the first attempt at standardization of IT portfolio management principles.

In peer-reviewed research, Christopher Verhoef has found that IT portfolios statistically behave more akin to biological populations than financial portfolios. Verhoef was general chair of the first convening of the new IEEE conference, "IEEE Equity," March 2007, which focuses on "quantitative methods for measuring, predicting, and understanding the relationship between IT and value."

Relationship to other IT Disciplines

IT portfolio management is an enabling technique for the objectives of IT Governance. It is related to both IT Service Management and Enterprise Architecture, and might even be seen as a bridge between the two. ITIL v3 calls for Service Portfolio Management which appears to be functionally equivalent.

MANAGEMENT INFORMATION SYSTEM

Management Information Systems (MIS), sometimes referred to as Information Management and Systems, is the discipline covering the application of people, technologies, and procedures-collectively called information systems-to solving business problems. Management Information

Systems are distinct from regular information systems in that they are used to analyze other information systems applied in operational activities in the organization. Academically, the term is commonly used to refer to the group of information management methods tied to the automation or support of human decision making, e.g. Decision Support Systems, Expert systems, and Executive information systems.

Background

In their infancy, business computers were used for the practical business of computing the payroll and keeping track of accounts payable and receivable. As applications were developed that provided managers with information about sales, inventories, and other data that would help in managing the enterprise, the term "MIS" arose to describe these kinds of applications. Today, the term is used broadly in a number of contexts and includes (but is not limited to): decision support systems, resource and people management applications, project management, and database retrieval applications.

Definition

The terms MIS and information system are often confused. Information systems include systems that are not intended for decision making. MIS is sometimes referred to, in a restrictive sense, as information technology management. That area of study should not be confused with computer science. IT service management is a practitioner-focused discipline. MIS has also some differences with Enterprise Resource Planning (ERP) as ERP incorporates elements that are not necessarily focused on decision support.

Alan Lee defines MIS as "...research in the information systems field examines more than just the technological system, or just the social system, or even the two side by side; in addition, it investigates the phenomena that emerge when the two interact."

BUSINESS PERFORMANCE MANAGEMENT

Business performance management (BPM) is a set of processes that help organizations optimize their business performance. It is a framework for organizing, automating and analyzing business methodologies, metrics, processes and systems that drive business performance.

BPM is seen as the next generation of business intelligence (BI). BPM helps businesses make efficient use of their financial, human, material and other resources.

History

An early reference to non-business performance management occurs in Sun Tzu's The Art of War. Sun Tzu claims that to succeed in war, one should have full knowledge of one's own strengths and weaknesses and full knowledge of one's enemy's strengths and weaknesses. Lack of either one might result in defeat. A certain school of thought draws parallels between the challenges in business and those of war, specifically:

- collecting data-both internal and external
- discerning patterns and meaning in the data (analyzing)
- responding to the resultant information

Prior to the start of the Information Age in the late 20th century, businesses sometimes took the trouble to laboriously collect data from non-automated sources. As they lacked computing resources to properly analyze the data they often made commercial decisions primarily on the basis of intuition.

As businesses started automating more and more systems, more and more data became available. However, collection remained a challenge due to a lack of infrastructure for data exchange or due to incompatibilities between systems.

Reports on the data gathered sometimes took months to generate. Such reports allowed informed long-term strategic decision-making. However, short-term tactical decision-making continued to rely on intuition.

In modern businesses, increasing standards, automation, and technologies have led to vast amounts of data becoming available.

Data warehouse technologies have set up repositories to store this data. Improved ETL and even recently Enterprise Application Integration tools have increased the speedy collecting of data.

OLAP reporting technologies have allowed faster generation of new reports which analyze the data. Business intelligence has now become the art of sieving through large amounts of data, extracting useful information and turning that information into actionable knowledge.

In 1989 Howard Dresner, a research analyst at Gartner, popularized "Business Intelligence" as an umbrella term to describe a set of concepts and methods to improve business decision-making by using fact-based support systems. Performance Management is built on a foundation of BI, but marries it to the planning and control cycle of the enterprise-with enterprise planning, consolidation and modeling capabilities.

The term "BPM" is now becoming confused with "Business Process Management", and many are converting to the term "Corporate Performance Management" or "Enterprise Performance Management".

What is BPM?

BPM involves consolidation of data from various sources, querying, and analysis of the data, and putting the results into practice.

BPM enhances processes by creating better feedback loops. Continuous and real-time reviews help to identify and eliminate problems before they grow. BPM's forecasting abilities help the company take corrective action in time to meet earnings projections. Forecasting is characterized by a high degree of predictability which is put into good use to answer what-if scenarios. BPM is useful in risk analysis and predicting outcomes of merger and acquisition scenarios and coming up with a plan to overcome potential problems.

BPM provides key performance indicators (KPIs) that help companies monitor efficiency of projects and employees against operational targets.

Metrics / Key Performance Indicators

For business data analysis to become a useful tool, however, it is essential that an enterprise understand its goals and objectives-essentially, that they know the direction in which they want the enterprise to progress. To help with this analysis key performance indicators (KPIs) are laid down to assess the present state of the business and to prescribe a course of action.

More and more organizations have started to speed up the availability of data. In the past, data only became available after a month or two, which did not help managers react swiftly enough. Recently, banks have tried to make data available at shorter intervals and have reduced delays.

For example, for businesses which have higher operational/credit risk loading (for example, credit cards and "wealth management"), A large multi-national bank makes KPI-related data available weekly, and sometimes offers a daily analysis of numbers and realtime dashboards are also provided.

This means data usually becomes available within 24 hours, necessitating automation and the use of IT systems.

Most of the time, BPM simply means use of several financial/nonfinancial metrics/key performance indicators to assess the present state of the business and to prescribe a course of action. Some of the areas from which top management analysis could gain knowledge by using BPM:

1. Customer-related numbers:
    1. New customers acquired
    2. Status of existing customers
    3. Attrition of customers (including breakup by reason for attrition)
2. Turnover generated by segments of the Customers-these could be demographic filters.
3. Outstanding balances held by segments of customers and terms of payment-these could be demographic filters.
4. Collection of bad debts within customer relationships.
5. Demographic analysis of individuals (potential customers) applying to become customers, and the levels of approval, rejections and pending numbers.
6. Delinquency analysis of customers behind on payments.
7. Profitability of customers by demographic segments and segmentation of customers by profitability.
8. Campaign management
9. Realtime Dashboard on Key operational metrics such

10. Clickstream analysis on a website
11. Key product portfolio trackers
12. Marketing Channel analysis
13. Sales Data analysis by product segments
14. Callcenter metrics

This is more an inclusive list than an exclusive one. The above more or less describes what a bank would do, but could also refer to a telephone company or similar service sector company.

What is important is:

1. KPI related data which is consistent, correct and provide an insight into operational aspects of a company.
2. Timely availability of KPI-related data.
3. KPIs designed to directly reflect the efficiency and effectiveness of a business
4. Information presented in a format which aids decision making for top management and decision makers
5. Ability to discern patterns or trends from organised information

BPM integrates the company's processes with CRM or ERP. Companies become able to gauge customer satisfaction, control customer trends and influence shareholder value.

Application Software Types

People working in business intelligence have developed tools that ease the work, especially when the intelligence task involves gathering and analyzing large amounts of unstructured data.

Tool categories commonly used for business performance management include:

- OLAP-Online Analytical Processing, sometimes simply called "Analytics" (based on dimensional analysis and the so-called "hypercube" or "cube")
- Scorecarding, dashboarding and data visualization
- Data warehouses
- Document warehouses
- Text mining
- DM-Data mining
- BPM-Business performance management
- EIS-Executive information systems
- DSS-Decision support systems
- MIS-Management information systems
- SEMS-Strategic Enterprise Management Software
- Business Dashboards

Designing and Implementing a Business Performance Management Programme

When implementing a BPM programme one might like to pose a number of questions and take a number of resultant decisions, such as:

- *Goal Alignment queries*: The first step is determining what the short and medium term purpose of the programme will be. What strategic goal(s) of the organization will be addressed by the programme? What organizational mission/vision does it relate to? A hypothesis needs to be crafted that details how this initiative will eventually improve results / performance (i.e. a strategy map).
- *Baseline queries*: Current information gathering competency needs to be assessed. Do we have the capability to monitor important sources of

information? What data is being collected and how is it being stored? What are the statistical parameters of this data, e.g., how much random variation does it contain? Is this being measured?

- *Cost and risk queries*: The financial consequences of a new BI initiative should be estimated. It is necessary to assess the cost of the present operations and the increase in costs associated with the BPM initiative? What is the risk that the initiative will fail? This risk assessment should be converted into a financial metric and included in the planning.
- *Customer and stakeholder queries*: Determine who will benefit from the initiative and who will pay. Who has a stake in the current procedure? What kinds of customers / stakeholders will benefit directly from this initiative? Who will benefit indirectly? What are the quantitative / qualitative benefits? Is the specified initiative the best way to increase satisfaction for all kinds of customers, or is there a better way? How will customer benefits be monitored? What about employees, shareholders, and distribution channel members?
- *Metrics-related queries*: These information requirements must be operationalized into clearly defined metrics. One must decide what metrics to use for each piece of information being gathered. Are these the best metrics? How do we know that? How many metrics need to be tracked? If this is a large number (it usually is), what kind of system can be used to track them? Are the metrics standardized, so they can be benchmarked against performance in other organizations? What are the industry standard metrics available?
- *Measurement Methodology-related queries*: One should establish a methodology or a procedure to

determine the best (or acceptable) way of measuring the required metrics. What methods will be used, and how frequently will data be collected? Are there any industry standards for this? Is this the best way to do the measurements? How do we know that?

- *Results-related queries*: The BPM programme should be monitored to ensure that objectives are being met. Adjustments in the programme may be necessary. The programme should be tested for accuracy, reliability, and validity. How can it be demonstrated that the BI initiative, and not something else, contributed to a change in results? How much of the change was probably random?

4

THE BUSINESS RULE

Business rules or business rulesets describe the operations, definitions and constraints that apply to an organization in achieving its goals. For example a business rule might state that no credit check is to be performed on return customers.

Others could define a tenant in terms of solvency or list preferred suppliers and supply schedules. These rules are then used to help the organization to better achieve goals, communicate among principals and agents, communicate between the organization and interested third parties, demonstrate fulfillment of legal obligations, operate more efficiently, automate operations, perform analysis on current practices, etc.

INTRODUCTION

Strategic management is distinct from business rules. Business rules are a means by which strategies are implemented. The rules tell an organization what it can do in detailed tactics, while the strategy tells it how to focus the business at a macro level to optimize results. Put differently, a strategy provides high-level direction about what an organization should do. Business rules can provide the tactical detail about exactly how a strategy will translate to actions.

Example business rule domains include:

- marketing strategies
- pricing policies
- customer relationship management practices
- human resources activities
- regulatory forces, either to ensure compliance with regulations, or to make decisions under regulations (e.g. determining someone's tax bill or whether they are eligible for a government benefit)
- product and service offerings or operation workflows.

HOW BUSINESS RULES ARE GATHERED

Business rules exist for an organization whether or not they are ever written down, talked about or even part of the organization's consciousness. However it is a fairly common practice for organizations to gather business rules in at least a very informal manner.

Organizations may choose to proactively describe their business practices in a database of rules. For example, they might hire a consultant to come through the organization to document and consolidate the various standards and methods currently in practice.

More commonly, business rules are discovered as part of a formal requirement gathering process during the initial stages of a project. In this case the collecting of the business rules are coincidental. Projects, such as the launching of a new product, might lead to a new body of business rules for an organization, i.e. this new product would require the employees to conceptualize about what the purpose of the organization is in a new way. This practice of coincidental business rule gathering is vulnerable to the creation of inconsistent or even conflicting business rules within different organizational units, or within the same organizational unit over time. Business Rules Methodology is the process of capturing business rules in English, in real-time while empowering users to manage rules with a few simple steps.

REAL WORLD APPLICATIONS AND OBSTACLES

Despite many software vendors, consultants and research institutions offering business rules solutions, business rules are usually only gathered when dictated by law, as the first step in the automation process or as an ephemeral aid to engineers. This is mostly due to the overhead and effort required to maintain this database of rules. This becomes most severe the more dynamic and fluid the business rules for an organization are, for example in start-up companies. Another factor mitigating usage is the lack of incentive for employees to part with their most valuable asset to the organization; their knowledge of the business rules. A third factor is access to viable technology for maintaining business rules. A classic solution is the business rules engine. Rules engine products have been gaining traction in the market place.

Software packages automate business rules using business logic. The term business rule is sometimes used interchangeably with business logic; however the latter connotes an engineering practice and the former an intrinsic business practice. There is value in outlining an organization's business rules regardless of whether this information is used to automate its operations.

Best Practices

1. *Declarative*: A business rule is a statement of truth about an organization. It is an attempt to describe the operations of an organization, not an attempt to prescribe how an organization should operate. This

is why business rules are said to be discovered or observed and not created.

2. *Atomic*: A rule is either completely true or completely false; there are no shades of gray. For example a rule for an airline that states passengers may upgrade to first class round-trip tickets if seats are available and they pay the fare increase does not imply that this deal is available for just one leg of the journey.
3. *Distinct, independent constructs*: Separate the things that define your business (the rules) from the processes (i.e. strategies and tactics). Don't build complex and cyclical dependencies-simplify and flatten the constructs.
4. *Expressed in natural language*: In order to appeal to the broadest audience, it is almost always best to express business rules in a natural language without the use of a lot of technical jargon.
5. *Business, not technology, oriented*: For example, a company's business rules should not be foreign to a knowledgeable customer.
6. *Business, not technology, owned*: Business rules come from business decisions. These are independent from implementation decisions.

Formal Specification

Business rules can be expressed in a very formal language. An example of when this rigour is required is in highly technical enterprises such as the building of a bridge. Another example is a project trying to automate the business rules gathering process. Example languages include Unified Modeling Language, Z notation, Business Process Execution Language, Web Services Policy Framework, Business Process Modeling Notation, or Semantics of Business Vocabulary and Business Rules (SBVR).

BUSINESS MODEL

The term business model describes a broad range of informal and formal models that are used by enterprises to represent various aspects of business, such as operational processes, organizational structures, and financial forecasts. Although the term can be traced to the 1950s, it achieved mainstream usage only in the 1990s. Many informal definitions of the term can be found in popular business literature, such as the following:

> *"A business model is a conceptual tool that contains a big set of elements and their relationships and allows expressing the business logic of a specific firm. It is a description of the value a company offers to one or several segments of customers and of the architecture of the firm and its network of partners for creating, marketing, and delivering this value and relationship capital, to generate profitable and sustainable revenue streams"-Osterwalder, Pigneur and Tucci (2005)*

More recently, researchers build definitions based on economic and organizational theories and show that the definitions are econometrically sound. For example, Malone, et al. (2006) at MIT propose an operational definition of business model, based on theories such as those from transaction cost economics. Zott and Amit (2002) from INSEAD and Wharton based their definition on boundary-spanning transactions.

Simply put: What problem does this business solve and how does it do so profitably?

COMPONENTS OF A BUSINESS MODEL

Many different conceptualizations of business models exist (Chesbrough and Rosenbloom 2000; Hamell 2000; Linder and Cantrell 2000; Petrovic, Kittl et al.; Weill and Vitale 2001; Gordijn 2002; Afuah and Tucci 2003;

Osterwalder 2004; Fetscherin & Knolmayer 2005). They all have various degrees of resemblance or difference. The model proposed by Osterwalder (2004) synthesises the different conceptualizations into a single reference model based on the similarities of a large range of models. The author's conceptualization describes a business model as consisting of nine related business model building blocks. Thus, a business model describes a company's business:

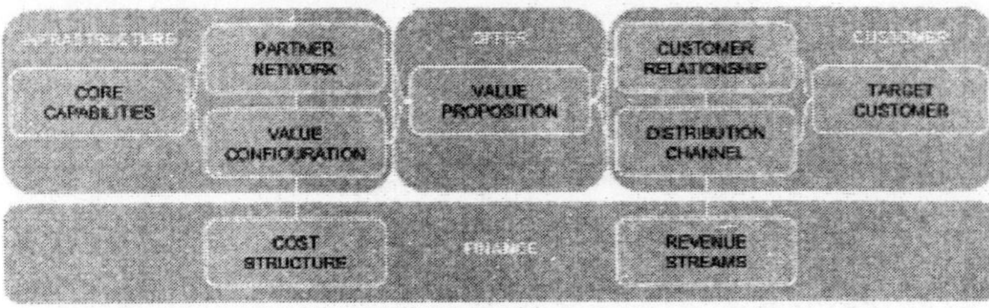

Infrastructure

- *Core capabilities*: The capabilities and competencies necessary to execute a company's business model.
- *Partner network*: The business alliances which complement other aspects of the business model.
- *Value configuration*: The rationale which makes a business mutually beneficial for a business and its customers.

Offering

- *Value proposition*: The products and services a business offers.

Customers

- *Target customer*: The target audience for a business' products and services.
- *Distribution channel*: The means by which a company delivers products and services to customers. This includes the company's marketing and distribution strategy.

- *Customer relationship*: The links a company establishes between itself and its different customer segments. The process of managing customer relationships is referred to as customer relationship management.

Finances

- *Cost structure*: The monetary consequences of the means employed in the business model. A company's DOC.
- *Revenue*: The way a company makes money through a variety of revenue flows. A company's income.

These 9 business model building blocks constitute a business model design template which allows companies to describe their business model.

Evolution

A brief history of the development of business models might run as follows. The oldest and most basic business model is the shop keeper model. This involves setting up a store in a location where potential customers are likely to be and displaying a product or service.

Over the years, business models have become much more sophisticated. The bait and hook business model (also referred to as the "razor and blades business model" or the "tied products business model") was introduced in the early 20th century. This involves offering a basic product at a very low cost, often at a loss (the "bait"), then charging compensatory recurring amounts for refills or associated products or services (the "hook"). Examples include: razor (bait) and blades (hook); cell phones (bait) and air time (hook); computer printers (bait) and ink cartridge refills (hook); and cameras (bait) and prints (hook). An interesting variant of this model is a software developer that gives away its word processor reader for free but charges several hundred dollars for its word processor writer.

In the 1950s, new business models came from McDonald's Restaurants and Toyota. In the 1960s, the innovators were Wal-Mart and Hypermarkets. The 1970s saw new business models from FedEx and Toys R Us; the 1980s from Blockbuster, Home Depot, Intel, and Dell Computer; the 1990s from Southwest Airlines, Netflix, eBay, Amazon.com, and Starbucks. Poorly thought out business models were a problem with many dot-coms.

Today, the type of business models might depend on how technology is used. For example, entrepreneurs on the internet have also created entirely new models that depend entirely on existing or emergent technology. Using technology, businesses can reach a large number of customers with minimal costs.

Example Business Models over the Years

- The open business model
- The subscription ousiness model
- The razor and blades business model (bait and hook)
- The pyramid scheme business model
- The multi-level marketing business model
- The network effects business model
- The monopolistic business model
- The cutting out the middleman model
- The auction business model
- The online auction business model
- The bricks and clicks business model
- The loyalty business models
- The Collective business models

- The industrialization of services business model
- The servitization of products business model
- The low-cost carrier business model
- The online content business model
- The freemium business model
- The premium business model
- The direct sales model
- The professional open-source model
- Various distribution business models

Do Business Models Matter?

Malone et al. (2006) at MIT find that some business models, as defined by them, indeed performed better than others in a dataset consisting of the largest U.S. firms, in the period 1998 through 2002.

Zott and Amit (2002) also link business models to performance, in the context of 190 young, growth-oriented firms in the US and Europe that had gone public between 1996 and 2000. See also their additional research on value drivers.

Business Model Innovation has become increasingly important as the recent IBM CEO survey 2006 shows. See also a video resource by Osterwalder (2006) on what the implications of business model innovation are and how it can be achieved.

Related Concepts

The process of business model design is part of business strategy. The implementation of a company's business model into organizational structures (e.g. organigrams, workflows, human resources) and systems (e.g. information technology architecture, production lines) is part of a company's business operations. It is important to understand that business modeling commonly refers to business process design at the operational level, whereas business models and business model design refer to defining the business logic of a company at the strategic level.

BUSINESS MODEL DESIGN

Business model design refers to the activity of designing a company's business model. It is part of the business development and business strategy process and involves design methods. Business model design includes the modeling and description of a company's:

- value propositions
- target customer segments
- distribution channels
- customer relationships
- value configurations
- core capabilities
- partner network
- cost structure
- revenue model

Business model design is distinct from business modeling. The former refers to defining the business logic of a company at the strategic level, whereas the latter refers to business process design at the operational level. A business model design template can facilitate the process of designing and describing a company's business model.

BUSINESS PLAN

This is a summary article that covers many topics related to business plans-their content, how they are used, legal issues, and spoofs of business plans, among others.-please see individual sections for links to detailed discussions of various topics relating to business plans.

A business plan is a formal statement of a set of business goals, the reasons why they are believed attainable, and the plan for reaching those goals. It may also contain background information about the organization or team attempting to reach those goals.

The business goals being attempted may be for-profit or non-profit. For-profit business plans typically focus on financial goals. Non-profit and government agency business plans tend to focus on service goals. Business plans may also target changes in perception and branding by the customer, client, tax-payer, or larger community. A business plan that has changes in perception and branding as its primary goals is called a marketing plan.

Business plans may be internally or externally focused. Externally focused plans target goals that are important to external stakeholders, particularly financial stakeholders. They typically have detailed information about the organization or team attempting to reach the goals. With for-profit entities, external stakeholders include investors and customers. External stake-holders of non-profits include donors and the clients of the non-profit's services. For government agencies, external stakeholders include tax-payers, higher-level government agencies, and international lending bodies such as the IMF, the World Bank, various economic agencies of the UN, and development banks.

Internally focused business plans target intermediate goals required to reach the external goals. They may cover the development of a new product, a new service, a new IT system, a restructuring of finance, the refurbishing of a factory or a restructuring of the organization. An internal business is often developed in conjunction with a balanced scorecard or a list of critical success factors. This allows success of the plan to be measured using non-financial measures. Business plans that identify and target internal goals, but provide only general guidance on how they will be met are called strategic plans.

Operational plans describe the goals of an internal organization, working group or department. Project plans, sometimes known as project frameworks, describe the goals of a particular project. They may also address the project's place within the organization's larger strategic goals.

Business Plan Content

Business plans are decision making tools. There is no fixed content for a business plan. Rather the content and format of the business plan is determined by the goals and audience. A business plan should contain whatever information is needed to decide whether or not to pursue a goal.

For example, a business plan for a non-profit might discuss the fit between the business plan and the organization's mission. Banks are quite concerned about defaults, so a business plan for a bank loan will build a convincing case for the organization's ability to repay the loan. Venture capitalists are primarily concerned about initial investment, feasibility, and exit valuation. A business plan for a project requiring equity financing will need to explain why current resources, upcoming growth opportunities, and sustainable competitive advantage will lead to a high exit valuation.

Preparing a business plan draws on a wide range of knowledge from many different business disciplines: finance, human resource management, intellectual property management, supply chain management, operations management, and marketing, among others. . It can be helpful to view the business plan as a collection of sub-plans, one for each of the main business disciplines.

Business Plan Preparation

Support Services

- books, portals, and other sources of written information
- consultancies
- electronic planning templates (software)
- face to face help: mentoring programs, training courses
  - — USA: SCORE, SBA centers
  - — Morocco: CRI (Centre Régional d'Investisment)
  - — England: Business Link
  - — Pakistan: SMEDA (Small and medium enterprise development authority)
  - — Other countries: needs research

RESOURCES FOR RESEARCHING FACTS AND FIGURES

Internal Corporate Records

Free Information

- published statistics on the web
- free articles and abstracts from consulting firms
- alumni resources-many undergraduate and graduate programs provide access to library and/or campus business center services as part of their package of alumni services.

Fee-based Services

- marketing reports from subscription services
- archive and journal services
- books

Strategic Analysis

- Industry Assessment
  - — The macroenvironment
  - — Customer Strategy & Market Analysis
- Competitor Analysis
  - — Porter 5 forces analysis

Forecasts: Modeling Techniques

Presentation Formats

The format of a business plan depends on its presentation context. It is not uncommon for businesses, especially start-ups to have three or four formats for the same business plan:

- an "elevator pitch"-a three minute summary of the business plan's executive summary. This is often used as a teaser to awaken the interest of potential funders, customers, or strategic partners.
- an oral presentation-a hopefully entertaining slide show and oral narrative that is meant to trigger discussion and interest potential investors in reading the written presentation. The content of the presentation is usually limited to the executive summary and a few key graphs showing financial trends and key decision making benchmarks. If a new product is being proposed and time permits, a demonstration of the product may also be included.
- a written presentation for external stakeholders-a detailed, well written, and pleasingly formatted plan targeted at external stakeholders.
- an internal operational plan-a detailed plan describing planning details that are needed by management but may not be of interest to external

stakeholders. Such plans have a somewhat higher degree of candor and informality than the version targeted at external stakeholders.

Revisiting the Business Plan

Cost Overruns and Revenue Shortfalls

Cost and revenue estimates are central to any business plan for deciding the viability of the planned venture. But costs are often underestimated and revenues overestimated resulting in later cost overruns, revenue shortfalls, and possibly non-viability. During the dot-com bubble 1997-2001 this was a problem for many technology start-ups. However, the problem is not limited to technology or the private sector; public works projects also routinely suffer from cost overruns and/or revenue shortfalls. The main causes of cost overruns and revenue shortfalls are optimism bias and strategic misrepresentation.

Legal and Liability Issues

Disclosure Requirements

An externally targeted business plan should list all legal concerns and financial liabilities that might negatively affect investors. Depending on the amount of funds being raised and the audience to whom the plan is presented, failure to do this may have severe legal consequences.

Limitations on Content and Audience

Non disclosure agreements (NDAs) with third parties, non-compete agreements, conflicts of interest, privacy concerns, and the protection of one's trade secrets may severely limit the audience to which one might show the business plan. Alternatively, they may require each party receiving the business plan to sign a contract accepting special clauses and conditions.

This situation is complicated by the fact that many venture capitalists will refuse to sign an NDA before looking at a business plan, lest it put them in the untenable position of looking at two independently developed look-alike business plans, both claiming originality.

In such situations one may need to develop two versions of the business plan: a stripped down plan that can be used to develop a relationship and a detail plan that is only shown when investors have sufficient interest and trust to sign an NDA.

How Business Plans are Used

Venture Capital

- business plan contests-provides a way for venture capitals to find promising projects
- venture capital assessment of business plans-focus on qualitative factors such as team.

Education

K-12

Business plans are used in some primary and secondary programs to teach economic principles.

Wikiversity has a v:Lunar Boom Town project where students of all ages can collaborate with designing and revising business models and practice evaluating them to learn practical business planning techniques and methodology.

Higher Education

- BA, MBA programs
  — integrative team projects
  — projects for specific course work
  — Business plan contests

Satires of Business Plans

The business plan is the subject of many satires. Satires are used both to express cynicism about business plans and as an educational tool to improve the quality of business plans. For example,

- Five Criteria for a successful business plan in biotech uses Dilbert comic strips to remind people of what not to do when researching and writing a business plan for a biotech start-up. Scott Adams, the author of Dilbert, is an MBA graduate (U.C. Berkeley) who sees humor as a critical tool that can improve the behavior of businesses and their managers. He has written numerous critiques of business practices, including business planning. The website Dilbert.com-Games has a mission statement generator that satires the wording often found in mission statements. His book The Dilbert Principle-A Cubicle's Eye View of Bosses, Meetings, Management Fads & Other Workplace Afflictions discusses the foibles of management and their plans as depicted in the Dilbert comic strips by Scott Adams.
- In the article "South Park's" Investing Lesson, the The Motley Fool columnist "Fool on the Hill" uses the Underpants Gnomes to illustrate the fallacy of focusing on goals without a clear implementation strategy. The Underpants Gnomes episode satires the business plans of the Dot.com era. It features a three-part business plan for a new coffee shop:

   1. Collect underpants
   2. Profit!

5

BUSINESS MARKETING

Marketing is a societal process that is needed to discern consumers' wants; focusing on a product/service to those wants, and to mould the consumers towards the products/services. Marketing is fundamental to any businesses growth. The marketing teams (Marketers) have the task to create the consumer awareness of the products/services through marketing techniques; if a business does not pay attention to their products/services and their consumers' demographics, the business would not be able to endure longevity.

Marketing tends to be seen as a creative industry, which includes advertising, distribution and selling. It is also concerned with anticipating the customers' future needs and wants, often through market research.

Its specialist areas include:

- Advertising and Branding
- Direct Marketing
- International Marketing
- Public Relations
- Communications
- Strategic Management
- Market Research

- Events Organisation
- Database Marketing
- Search Engine Marketing

INTRODUCTION

A market-focused, or customer-focused, organization first determines what its potential customers desire, and then builds the product or service. Marketing theory and practice is justified in the belief that customers use a product or service because they have a need, or because it provides a perceived benefit.

Two major factors of marketing are the recruitment of new customers (acquisition) and the retention and expansion of relationships with existing customers (base management). Once a marketer has converted the prospective buyer, base management marketing takes over. The process for base management shifts the marketer to building a relationship, nurturing the links, enhancing the benefits that sold the buyer in the first place, and improving the product/service continuously to protect the business from competitive encroachments.

For a marketing plan to be successful, the mix of the four "Ps" must reflect the wants and desires of the consumers in the target market. Trying to convince a market segment to buy something they don't want is extremely expensive and seldom successful. Marketers depend on marketing research, both formal and informal, to determine what consumers want and what they are willing to pay for it. Marketers hope that this process will give them a sustainable competitive advantage. Marketing management is the practical application of this process. The offer is also an important addition to the 4P's theory.

Within most organizations, the activities encompassed by the marketing function are led by a Vice President or

Director of Marketing. A growing number of organizations, especially large US companies, have a Chief Marketing Officer position, reporting to the Chief Executive Officer.

The American Marketing Association (AMA) states, "Marketing is the process of planning and executing the conception, pricing, promotion, and distribution of ideas, goods, and services to create exchanges that satisfy individual and organizational objectives".

Marketing methods are informed by many of the social sciences, particularly psychology, sociology, and economics. Anthropology is also a small, but growing, influence. Market research underpins these activities. Through advertising, it is also related to many of the creative arts. Marketing is a wide and heavily interconnected subject with extensive publications. It is also an area of activity infamous for re-inventing itself and its vocabulary according to the times and the culture.

Marketing is a very essential part of any business.

Two Levels of Marketing

Strategic Marketing attempts to determine how an organization competes against its competitors in a market place. In particular, it aims at generating a competitive advantage relative to its competitors.

Operational Marketing executes marketing functions to attract and keep customers and to maximize the value derived for them, as well as to satisfy the customer with prompt services and meeting the customer expectations. Operational Marketing includes the determination of the marketing mix.

Four Ps

In popular usage, "marketing" is the promotion of products, especially advertising and branding. However, in professional usage the term has a wider meaning which recognizes that marketing is customer centered. Products are often developed to meet the desires of groups of customers or even, in some cases, for specific customers. E. Jerome McCarthy divided marketing into four general sets of activities. His typology has become so universally recognized that his four activity sets, the Four Ps, have passed into the language.

The four Ps are:

- Product: The product aspects of marketing deal with the specifications of the actual goods or services, and how it relates to the end-user's needs and wants. The scope of a product generally includes supporting elements such as warranties, guarantees, and support.
- Pricing: This refers to the process of setting a price for a product, including discounts. The price need not be monetary-it can simply be what is exchanged for the product or services, e.g. time, energy, psychology or attention.
- Promotion: This includes advertising, sales promotion, publicity, and personal selling, and refers to the various methods of promoting the product, brand, or company.
- Placement or distribution refers to how the product gets to the customer; for example, point of sale placement or retailing. This fourth P has also sometimes been called Place, referring to the channel by which a product or services is sold (e.g. online vs. retail), which geographic region or industry, to which segment (young adults, families, business people), etc.

These four elements are often referred to as the marketing mix, which a marketer can use to craft a marketing plan. The four Ps model is most useful when marketing low value consumer products. Industrial products, services, high value consumer products require adjustments to this model. Services marketing must account for the unique nature of services. Industrial or B2B marketing must account for the long term contractual agreements that are typical in supply chain transactions. Relationship marketing attempts to do this by looking at marketing from a long term relationship perspective rather than individual transactions. As a counter to this, Morgan, in Riding the Waves of Change (Jossey-Bass, 1988), suggests that one of the greatest limitations of the 4 Ps approach "is that it unconsciously emphasizes the inside-out view (looking from the company outwards), whereas the essence of marketing should be the outside-in approach". Nevertheless, the 4 Ps offer a memorable and workable guide to the major categories of marketing activity, as well as a framework within which these can be used.

Seven Ps

As well as the standard four Ps (Product, Pricing, Promotion and Place), services marketing calls upon an extra three, totaling seven and known together as the extended marketing mix. These are:

- *People*: Any person coming into contact with customers can have an impact on overall satisfaction. Whether as part of a supporting service to a product or involved in a total service, people are particularly important because, in the customer's eyes, they are generally inseparable from the total service. As a result of this, they must be appropriately trained, well motivated and the right type of person. Fellow customers are also sometimes referred to under 'people', as they too can affect the customer's service experience, (e.g., at a sporting event).

- *Process*: This is the process(es) involved in providing a service and the behaviour of people, which can be crucial to customer satisfaction.
- *Physical evidence*: Unlike a product, a service cannot be experienced before it is delivered, which makes it intangible. This, therefore, means that potential customers could perceive greater risk when deciding whether to use a service. To reduce the feeling of risk, thus improving the chance for success, it is often vital to offer potential customers the chance to see what a service would be like. This is done by providing physical evidence, such as case studies, testimonials or demonstrations.

Web 2.0 and Marketing New 4Ps

The original 4Ps concept idea was developed to help marketers manage the four most important aspect of marketing. With the Internet and the Web 2.0, marketers have needed to adapt a broader perspective on these elements. Idris Mootee devised a "New 4Ps" model in 2001 to supplement the traditional marketing 4Ps. They are Personalization, Participation, Peer-to-Peer and Predictive Modeling.

- *Personalization*: The author here refers to customization of products and services through the use of the Internet. Early examples include Dell on-line and Amazon.com, but this concept is further extended with emerging social media and advanced algorithms. Emerging technologies will continue to push this idea forward.
- *Participation*: This is to allow customer to participate in what the brand should stand for; what should be the product directions and even which ads to run. This concept is laying the foundation for disruptive change through democratization of information.

- *Peer-to-Peer*': This refers to customer networks and communities where advocacy happens. The historical problem with marketing is that it is "interruptive" in nature, trying to impose a brand on the customer. This is most apparent in TV advertising. These "passive customer bases" will ultimately be replaced by the "active customer communities". Brand engagement happens within those conversations. P2P is now being referred as Social Computing and will likely to be the most disruptive force in the future of marketing.
- *Predictive modeling*: This refers to predictive algorithms, such as neural network, that are being successfully applied in marketing problems (both a regression as well as a classification problem).

Product

Scope

- Breadth--number of product lines in a range.
- Depth--number of product items in a product line.

Steps in Product Design

- Design and development of product ideas.
- Selection of and sifting through product ideas.
- Design and testing of product concept.
- Analysis of profitability of product concept.
- Design and testing of physical product.

Packaging and Trademarks

Requirements of Good Packaging

- Appropriately designed for target market
- Eye-catching

- Suitable to product
- Compliant with retailers' requirements
- Promotes image of enterprise
- Distinguishable from competitors' products
- Strong, convenient, well-designed
- Point of difference in service and supply of product.

Forms of Packaging

- Specialty packaging-emphasizes the elegant character of the product
- Packaging for double-use
- Combination packaging two or more products packaged in the same container
- Kaleidoscopic packaging-packaging changes continually to reflect a series or particular theme
- Packaging for immediate consumption-to be thrown away after use
- Packaging for resale-packed, into appropriate quantities, for the retailer or wholesaler

Significance of a Trademark

- Distinguishes one company's goods from those of another
- Serves as advertisement for quality
- Protects both consumers and manufacturers
- Used in displays and advertising campaigns
- Used to market new products

Requirements of a Good Trademark

- Reflects products' advantages
- Good, simple language

- Easily pronounced and remembered
- Distinct from names of other products
- Easily added to an existing range
- Easily registered for legal protection

Pricing

Pricing refers to the amount of money exchanged for a product. This value is determined by utility to the consumer in terms of money and/or sacrifice that he is prepared to give for it.

Objectives

- Definite sales volume
- Achieve profit
- Larger market share
- Maintain market share
- Eliminate competition
- Advantages of mass production
- Satisfactory return on capital

Factors Influencing Price-determination

- Production and distribution costs
- Substitute goods available
- Normal trade practices
- Fixed prices
- Reaction of distributors
- Reaction of consumers
- Nature of demand:
  - — Elastic
  - — Inelastic

- Form of market:
— Perfect competition
— Monopolistic competition
— Monopoly
— Oligopoly

Steps to Determine Price

- Determine market share to be captured
- Set up price strategy
- Estimate demand
- Evaluate competitors' reactions

Distribution

Channels

- Manufacturer to consumer (most direct)
- Manufacturer to wholesaler to retailer to consumer (traditional)
- Manufacturer to agent to retailer to consumer (current)
- Manufacturer to agent to wholesaler to retailer to consumer
- Manufacturer to agent to customer (ex: AMWAY)

Manufacturers

Reasons for Direct Selling Methods

- Manufacturer wants to demonstrate goods.
- Wholesalers, retailers and agents not actively selling.
- Manufacturer unable to convince wholesalers or retailers to stock product.
- High profit margin added to goods by wholesalers and retailers.
- Middlemen unable to transport.

Reasons for Indirect Selling Methods

- Manufacturer does not have the financial resources to distribute goods.
- Distribution channels already established.
- Manufacturer has no knowledge of efficient distribution.
- Manufacturer wishes to use capital for further production.
- Too many consumers in a large area; difficult to reach.
- Manufacturer does not have a wide assortment of goods to enable efficient marketing.

Wholesalers

Reasons for using Wholesalers

- Bear risk of selling goods to retailer or consumer
- Storage space
- Decrease transport costs
- Grant credit to retailers
- Able to sell for the manufacturers
- Give advice to manufacturers
- Break down products into smaller quantities

Reasons for Bypassing Wholesalers

- Limited storage facilities
- Retailers' preferences
- Wholesaler cannot promote products successfully
- Development of wholesalers' own brands
- Desire for closer market contact
- Position of power

- Cost of wholesalers' services
- Price stabilisation
- Need for rapid distribution
- Make more money

Ways of Bypassing Wholesalers

- Sales offices or branches
- Mail orders
- Direct sales to retailers
- Travelling agents
- Direct Orders

Agents

- Commission agents work for anyone who needs their services. They do not acquire ownership of goods but receive del credere commission.
- Selling agents act on an extended contractual basis, selling all of the products of the manufacturer. They have full authority regarding price and terms of sale.
- Buying agents buy goods on behalf of producers and retailers. They have an expert knowledge of the purchasing function.
- Brokers specialize in the sale of one specific product. They receive a brokerage.
- Factory representatives represent more than one manufacturer. They operate within a specific area and sell related lines of goods but have limited authority regarding price and sales terms.

Marketing Communications

Marketing communications breaks down the strategies involved with marketing messages into categories based on the goals of each message. There are distinct stages in converting strangers to customers that govern the communication medium that should be used.

Advertising

- Paid form of public presentation and expressive promotion of ideas
- Aimed at masses
- Manufacturer may determine what goes into advertisement
- Pervasive and impersonal medium

Functions and Advantages of Successful Advertising

- Task of the salesman made easier
- Forces manufacturer to live up to conveyed image
- Protects and warns customers against false claims and inferior products
- Enables manufacturer to mass-produce product
- Continuous reminder
- Uninterrupted production a possibility
- Increases goodwill
- Raises standards of living (or perceptions thereof)
- Prices decrease with increased popularity
- Educates manufacturer and wholesaler about competitors' offerings as well as shortcomings in their own.

Objectives

- Maintain demand for well-known goods
- Introduce new and unknown goods
- Increase demand for well-known goods

Requirements of a Good Advertisement

- Attract attention
- Stimulate interest
- Create a desire
- Bring about action
- Create Awareness

Eight Steps in an Advertising Campaign

- Market research
- Setting out aims
- Budgeting
- Choice of media (TV,newspaper,radio)
- Choice of actors (New Trend)
- Design and wording
- Coordination
- Test results

Personal Sales

Oral presentation given by a salesman who approaches individuals or a group of potential customers:

- Live, interactive relationship
- Personal interest
- Attention and response

Sales Promotion

Short-term incentives to encourage buying of products:

- Instant appeal
- Anxiety to sell

Publicity

- Stimulation of demand through press release giving a favourable report to a product

- Higher degree of credibility
- Effectively news
- Boosts enterprise's image

Customer Focus

Many companies today have a customer focus (or customer orientation). This implies that the company focuses its activities and products on consumer demands. Generally there are three ways of doing this: the customer-driven approach, the sense of identifying market changes and the product innovation approach.

In the consumer-driven approach, consumer wants are the drivers of all strategic marketing decisions. No strategy is pursued until it passes the test of consumer research. Every aspect of a market offering, including the nature of the product itself, is driven by the needs of potential consumers. The starting point is always the consumer. The rationale for this approach is that there is no point spending R&D funds developing products that people will not buy. History attests to many products that were commercial failures in spite of being technological breakthroughs.

A formal approach to this customer-focused marketing is known as SIVA (Solution, Information, Value, Access). This system is basically the four Ps renamed and reworded to provide a customer focus.

The SIVA Model provides a demand/customer centric version alternative tc the well-known 4Ps supply side model (product, price, place, promotion) of marketing management.

Product-> Solution

Promotion-> Information

Price-> Value

Place->Access

The four elements of the SIVA model are:

1. *Solution*: How appropriate is the solution to the customers problem/need?
2. *Information*: Does the customer know about the solution, and if so how, who from, do they know enough to let them make a buying decision?
3. *Value*: Does the customer know the value of the transaction, what it will cost, what are the benefits, what might they have to sacrifice, what will be their reward?
4. *Access*: Where can the customer find the solution? How easily/locally/remotely can they buy it and take delivery?

This model was proposed by Chekitan Dev and Don Schultz in the Marketing Management Journal of the American Marketing Association, and presented by them in Market Leader-the journal of the Marketing Society in the UK.

The model focuses heavily on the customer and how they view the transaction.

Product Focus

In a product innovation approach, the company pursues product innovation, then tries to develop a market for the product. Product innovation drives the process and marketing research is conducted primarily to ensure that a profitable market segment(s) exists for the innovation. The rationale is that customers may not know what options will be available to them in the future so we should not expect them to tell us what they will buy in the future. However, marketers can aggressively over-pursue product innovation and try to overcapitalize on a niche. When pursuing a product innovation approach, marketers must ensure that they have a varied and multi-tiered approach to product innovation. It is claimed that if Thomas Edison depended on marketing research he would have produced larger candles rather than inventing light bulbs. Many firms, such as research and development focused companies, successfully focus on product innovation (Such as Nintendo who constantly change the way Video games are played). Many purists doubt whether this is really a form of marketing orientation at all, because of the ex post status of consumer research. Some even question whether it is marketing.

- An emerging area of study and practice concerns internal marketing, or how employees are trained and managed to deliver the brand in a way that positively impacts the acquisition and retention of customers (employer branding).
- Diffusion of innovations research explores how and why people adopt new products, services and ideas.
- A relatively new form of marketing uses the Internet and is called internet marketing or more generally e-marketing, affiliate marketing, desktop advertising or online marketing. It typically tries to perfect the segmentation strategy used in traditional marketing. It targets its audience more precisely, and is sometimes called personalized marketing or one-to-one marketing.
- With consumers' eroding attention span and willingness to give time to advertising messages, marketers are turning to forms of Permission marketing such as Branded content, Custom media and Reality marketing.
- The use of herd behavior in marketing.

In an article entitled "Swarming the shelves: How shops can exploit people's herd mentality to increase sales", The Economist recently reported a recent conference in Rome on the subject of the simulation of adaptive human behavior. Mechanisms to increase impulse buying and get people "to buy more by playing on the herd instinct" were shared. The basic idea is that people will buy more of products that are seen to be popular, and several feedback mechanisms to get product popularity information to consumers are mentioned, including smart-cart technology and the use of Radio Frequency Identification Tag technology. A "swarm-moves" model was introduced by a Princeton researcher, which is appealing to supermarkets because it can "increase sales without the need to give people discounts." Large retailers Wal-Mart in the United States and Tesco in Britain plan to test the technology in spring 2007.

Other recent studies on the "power of social influence" include an "artificial music market in which some 14,000 people downloaded previously unknown songs" (Columbia University, New York); a Japanese chain of convenience stores which orders its products based on "sales data from department stores and research companies;" a Massachusetts company exploiting knowledge of social networking to improve sales; and online retailers who are increasingly informing consumers about "which products are popular with like-minded consumers" (e.g., Amazon, eBay).

CRITICISM OF MARKETING

Some aspects of marketing, especially promotion, are the subject of criticism. It is especially problematic in classical economic theory, which is based on the assumption that supply and demand are independent. However, product promotion is an attempt coming from the supply side to influence demand. In this way producer market power is attained as measured by profits that would not be realized under a free market. Then the argument follows that non-free markets are imperfect and lead to production and consumption of suboptimal amounts of the product. Critics acknowledge that marketing has legitimate uses in connecting goods and services to the consumers who want them. Critics also point out that marketing techniques have been used to achieve morally dubious ends by businesses, governments and criminals. Critics see a systemic social evil inherent in marketing (see No Logo, Bill Hicks, Marxism or Commercial Alert). Marketing is accused of creating ruthless exploitation of both consumers and workers by treating people as commodities whose purpose is to consume. (see Fashion victim)

Most marketers believe that marketing techniques themselves are amoral. While it is ethically neutral, it can be used for negative purposes, such as selling unhealthy food to obese people or selling SUVs in a time of global warming, but it can also have a positive influence on consumer welfare.

The Observer's survey among 1,206 UK adult consumers in 2001 highlighted some of the stark changes our society has gone through in the last two decades. This raises a question on the effectiveness of the CIM's definition of marketing (anticipating, identifying and satisfying customer needs profitably), mainly in consumer marketing. There are similar concerns in industrial markets, also known as business-to-business or B2B. Industrial market segmentation attempts to provide some answers.

Core marketing elements such as segmentation, targeting and positioning are still relevant in the modern (or post-modern) world. However, they are complex topics that need a high level of effort, intelligent thinking as well as resources to be implemented successfully. A definitive statement cannot be made whether the conventional marketing concept is applicable in today's environment. Its relevance is very much situational and depends on many factors such as the product, the segment, time, location, political and economic conditions and the inner workings of a company.

However, some scholars such as Stephen Brown challenge the marketing concept in an extreme language. Their statements, sometimes unfair, are relevant, which is why Post-Modern Marketing 2 was chosen as a key reference point for this chapter.

On the one hand Brown makes positive statements about marketing, e.g. "marketing is endowed with considerable personal charm and has enjoyed more than its fair share of conquests" (Brown, 1998:16); and "indeed, the increasing academic attention that is being devoted to marketing and consumption-related phenomena by non-business disciplines such as sociology, anthropology and history; far from being the second-hand rose of the scholarship, marketing is now something of a fashion leader" (p 17)

On the other hand, he condemns marketing by saying "marketing has to decide whether to expose its intellectual nakedness or press itself against the searing heat of postmodernism" (p 17); and using quotes such as "mid-life crisis" (p 23); "in decline; failing; anachronistic; being abandoned; no longer appropriate; in an unprecedented state of crisis; delivered nothing of value; failure; confusion; misunderstanding; occasional inexplicable hitting of the jackpot" (p. 21).

This apparent love-hate relationship is proof in itself that even a skeptics find it difficult to deny the contribution that marketing has made and can make to customer satisfaction and economic value. It has contributed to both customers' and suppliers' quality of life by selecting profitable customer satisfaction as its sole objective. The marketing concept, together with other business disciplines, helped the UK to make the transition from a 19th-century manufacturing economy to a modern model of success in the service industry, creating an economic growth period never seen before in the United Kingdom.

Marketing has helped create value through customized products, no-questions-asked refund policies, comfortable cars, environmental attention, shopkeepers' smile, and guaranteed delivery dates. Even some government departments address the public not as 'the Queen's subjects' or 'the applicants' any more but as 'customers.' Of course all of the above is done for economic or political gain, for better or worse. Despite all this achievement, to dismiss marketing as a failure is unfair.

Marketing also helps companies avoid unnecessary R&D, operational and sales costs by helping to develop products because customers want them, not for the sake of innovation. Another success is the now commonly implemented value-pricing principle, whereby a product or service is sold for the price the customer is willing to pay, not on a cost-plus basis. This way, both suppliers and customers get a fair deal.

In the context of segmentation, Brown suggests that "the traditional, linear, step-by-step marketing model of analysis, planning, implementation and control no longer seems applicable, appropriate or even pertinent to what is actually happening on the ground" (p. 23-24). If Mr. Brown had studied "the ground" before making his statement, he would have realised that companies are successful the world over precisely because they implement this model.

They segment their markets, relate their products and services to them, define their value proposition and serve their customers accordingly. Examples are General Electric, HSBC, PriceWaterhouseCoopers, Smiths Aerospace, BAE Systems, BOC Edwards, Weir Group and the BT Group to name but a few. A brief visit to their websites can make this point clear. Stephen Brown also has a constructive suggestion: "I reckon we need more passion in marketing, not less; it is time we banished banishing passion from works of marketing scholarship" (p. 256). This refers mainly to promotion, which is only one element within the marketing concept. The truth is that marketing today leads the way in segmentation, innovation, pricing, product management, distribution, and last but not least, promotion.

After all the contribution as well as further potential, to deny its successes and try to reduce it to only promotion is a great injustice to the marketing profession as well as to academic insight. Contrary to Brown's suggestion in his final paragraph (p. 257), we need objectivity, rigour, quantification, models, relationships, paradigm shifts and (some application of) science.

Construction Marketing

Due to increased competition, privatisation and globalisation, marketing and business development have become increasingly important functions in all construction organisations. Marketing research, corporate branding and public relations are increasingly being seen as vital in a marketplace typified by sophisticated and demanding clients and customers, and a socially and environmentally aware general public and media.

STRATEGIC PLANNING

Strategic planning is an organization's process of defining its strategy, or direction, and making decisions on allocating its resources to pursue this strategy, including its capital and people. Various business analysis techniques can be used in strategic planning, including SWOT analysis and PEST analysis. The outcome is normally a strategic plan which is used as guidance to define functional and divisional plans, including Technology, Marketing, etc.

Strategic Planning is the formal consideration of an organization's future course. All strategic planning deals with at least one of three key questions:

1. "What do we do?"

2. "For whom do we do it?"

3. "How do we excel?"

In business strategic planning, the third question is better phrased "How can we beat or avoid competition?"

In many organizations, this is viewed as a process for determining where an organization is going over the next year or more-typically 3 to 5 years, although some extend their vision to 20 years.

In order to determine where it is going, the organization needs to know exactly where it stands, then determines where it wants to go and how it will get there. The resulting document is called the "strategic plan".

It is also true that strategic planning may be a tool for effectively plotting the direction of a company; however, strategic planning itself cannot foretell exactly how the market will evolve and what issues will surface in the coming days in order to plan your organizational strategy. Therefore, strategic innovation and tinkering with the 'strategic plan' have to be a cornerstone strategy for an organization to survive the turbulent business climate. (Ziaur Rahman, IITM, iitmbd.org, Dhaka)

Vision, Mission and Values

Vision: Defines where the organization wants to be in the future. It reflects the optimistic view of the organization's future.

Mission: Defines where the organization is going now, basically describing the purpose, why this organization exists.

Values: Main values protected by the organization during the progression, reflecting the organization's culture and priorities. Strategic planning saves time, every minute spent in planning saves ten minutes in execution.

The purpose of individual strategic planning is for you to increase your return on energy, the return on the mental, emotional, physical and spiritual capital you have invested in your life and career.

Every minute an individual spends planning their goals, activities and time in advance saves ten minutes of work in the execution of those plans. Careful advance planning gives you a return of ten times, or 1,000%, on your investment of mental, emotional and physical energy. (The 100 Absolutely Unbreakable Laws of Business Success.)

Methodologies

There are many approaches to strategic planning but typically a three-step process may be used:

- Situation-evaluate the current situation and how it came about.
- Target-define goals and/or objectives (sometimes called ideal state)
- Path-map a possible route to the goals/objectives

One alternative approach is called Draw-See-Think

- Draw-what is the ideal image or the desired end state?
- See-what is today's situation? What is the gap from ideal and why?
- Think-what specific actions must be taken to close the gap between today's situation and the ideal state?
- Plan-what resources are required to execute the activities?

An alternative to the Draw-See-Think approach is called See-Think-Draw

- See-what is today's situation?
- Think-define goals/objectives
- Draw-map a route to achieving the goals/objectives

In other terms strategic planning can be as follows:

- Vision-Define the vision and set a mission statement with hierarchy of goals
- SWOT-According to the desired goals conduct analysis
- Formulate-Formulate actions and processes to be taken to attain these goals
- Implement-Implementation of the agreed upon processes
- Control-Monitor and get feedback from implemented processes to fully control the operation

Situational Analysis

When developing strategies, analysis of the organization and its environment as it is at the moment and how it may develop in the future, is important. The analysis has to be executed at an internal level as well as an external level to identify all opportunities and threats of the new strategy. There are several factors to assess in the external situation analysis:

1. Markets (customers)
2. Competition
3. Technology
4. Supplier markets
5. Labor markets
6. The economy
7. The regulatory environment

It is rare to find all seven of these factors having critical importance. It is also uncommon to find that the first two-markets and competition-are not of critical importance. (Bradford "External Situation-What to Consider")

Analysis of the external environment normally focuses on the customer. Management should be visionary in formulating customer strategy, and should do so by thinking about market environment shifts, how these could impact customer sets, and whether those customer sets are the ones the company wishes to serve.

Analysis of the competitive environment is also performed, many times based on the framework suggested by Michael Porter.

Goals, Objectives and Targets

Strategic planning is a very important business activity. It is also important in the public sector areas such as education. It is practiced widely informally and formally. Strategic planning and decision processes should end with objectives and a roadmap of ways to achieve those objectives.

The following terms have been used in Strategic Planning: desired end states, plans, policies, goals, objectives, strategies, tactics and actions. Definitions vary, overlap and fail to achieve clarity. The most common of these concepts are specific, time bound statements of intended future results and general and continuing statements of intended future results, which most models refer to as either goals or objectives (sometimes interchangeably).

One model of organizing objectives uses hierarchies. The items listed above may be organized in a hierarchy of means and ends and numbered as follows: Top Rank Objective (TRO), Second Rank Objective, Third Rank Objective, etc. From any rank, the objective in a lower rank answers to the question "How?" and the objective in a higher rank answers to the question "Why?" The exception is the Top Rank Objective (TRO): there is no answer to the "Why?" question. That is how the TRO is defined.

People typically have several goals at the same time. "Goal congruency" refers to how well the goals combine with each other. Does goal A appear compatible with goal B? Do they fit together to form a unified strategy? "Goal hierarchy" consists of the nesting of one or more goals within other goal(s).

One approach recommends having short-term goals, medium-term goals, and long-term goals. In this model, one can expect to attain short-term goals fairly easily: they stand just slightly above one's reach. At the other extreme, long-term goals appear very difficult, almost impossible to attain. Strategic management jargon sometimes refers to "Big Hairy Audacious Goals" (BHAGs) in this context.) Using one goal as a stepping-stone to the next involves goal sequencing.

A person or group starts by attaining the easy short-term goals, then steps up to the medium-term, then to the long-term goals. Goal sequencing can create a "goal stairway". In an organizational setting, the organization may co-ordinate goals so that they do not conflict with each other. The goals of one part of the organization should mesh compatibly with those of other parts of the organization.

Mission Statements and Vision Statements

Organizations sometimes summarize goals and objectives into a mission statement and/or a vision statement:

While the existence of a shared mission is extremely useful, many strategy specialists question the requirement for a written mission statement. However, there are many models of strategic planning that start with mission statements, so it is useful to examine them here.

- *A Mission statement*: tells you what the company is now. It concentrates on present; it defines the customer(s), critical processes and it informs you about the desired level of performance.
- *A Vision statement*: outlines what a company wants to be. It concentrates on future; it is a source of inspiration; it provides clear decision-making criteria.

Many people mistake vision statement for mission statement. The Vision describes a future identity and the Mission describes why it will be achieved. A Mission statement defines the purpose or broader goal for being in existence or in the business. It serves as an ongoing guide without time frame. The mission can remain the same for decades if crafted well. Vision is more specific in terms of objective and future state. Vision is related to some form of achievement if successful.

A mission statement can resemble a vision statement in a few companies, but that can be a grave mistake. It can confuse people. The vision statement can galvanize the people to achieve defined objectives, even if they are stretch objectives, provided the vision is SMART (Specific, Measurable, Achievable, Relevant and Timebound). A mission statement provides a path to realize the vision in line with its values. These statements have a direct bearing on the bottomline and success of the organization.

Which comes first? The mission statement or the vision statement? That depends. If you have a new start up business, new program or plan to re engineer your current services, then the vision will guide the mission statement and the rest of the strategic plan. If you have an established business where the mission is established, then many times, the mission guides the vision statement and the rest of the strategic plan. Either way, you need to know where you are, your current resources, your current obstacles, and where you want to go-the vision for the future. Features of an effective vision statement may include:

- Clarity and lack of ambiguity
- Paint a vivid and clear picture, not ambiguous
- Describing a bright future (hope)
- Memorable and engaging expression
- Realistic aspirations, achievable
- Alignment with organizational values and culture, Rational
- Time bound if it talks of achieving any goal or objective

To become really effective, an organizational vision statement must (the theory states) become assimilated into the organization's culture.

Leaders have the responsibility of communicating the vision regularly, creating narratives that illustrate the vision, acting as role-models by embodying the vision, creating short-term objectives compatible with the vision, and encouraging others to craft their own personal vision compatible with the organization's overall vision.

VALUE MIGRATION

Adrian Slywotzky describes Value migration in his book, Value Migration: How to Think Several Moves Ahead of the Competition, as the shifting of value-creating forces. Value migrates from outmoded business models to business designs that are better able to satisfy customers' priorities.

Three Types

- Value flows between industries-example: from airlines to entertainment
- Value flows between companies-example: from Corel WordPerfect to Microsoft

- Value flows between business designs within a company-example: from IBM mainframe computers to IBM PC's with system integration

Three Stages

- Value inflow stage-value is absorbed from other companies or industries
- Value stability stage-competitive equilibrium with stable market shares and stable profit margins
- Value outflow stage-companies lose value to other parts of the industry-reduced profit margins-loss of market share-outflow of talent and other resources

The value chain is the sum of all activities that add utility to the customer. Parts of the value chain will be internal to the company, while others will come from suppliers, distributors, and other channel partners. A linkage occurs whenever one activity affects other activities in the chain. To optimize a value chain, the linkages must be well coordinated.

The calculation of value migration is more difficult than it would at first seem. Value is perceived by customers and, as such, is subjective. This is very difficult to measure so relative market value of the firm is used as a proxy. Relative market value (defined as capitalization divided by annual revenue) is used as an indication of the firms success at creating value.

COMPETITIVE ADVANTAGE

Competitive advantage (CA) is a position that a firm occupies in its competitive landscape. Michael Porter posits that a competitive advantage, sustainable or not, exists when a company makes economic rents, that is, their earnings exceed their costs (including cost of capital). That means that normal competitive pressures are not able to drive down the firm's earnings to the point where they cover all costs and just provide minimum sufficient additional return to keep capital invested. Most forms of competitive advantage cannot be sustained for any length of time because the promise of economic rents drives competitors to duplicate the competitive advantage held by any one firm.

A firm possesses a Sustainable Competitive Advantage (SCA) when it has value-creating processes and positions that cannot be duplicated or imitated by other firms that lead to the production of above normal rents. An SCA is different from a competitive advantage (CA) in that it provides a long-term advantage that is not easily replicated. But these above-normal rents can attract new entrants who drive down economic rents. A CA is a position a firm attains that lead to above-normal rents or a superior financial performance. The processes and positions that engender such a position are not necessarily non-duplicable or inimitable.

Analysis of the factors of profitability is the subject of numerous theories of strategy including the five forces model pioneered by Michael Porter of the Harvard Business School.

In marketing and strategic management, sustainable competitive advantage is an advantage that one firm has relative to competing firms. The source of the advantage can be something the company does that is distinctive and difficult to replicate, also known as a core competency--for example Procter & Gamble's ability to derive superior consumer insights and implement them in managing its brand portfolio. It can also be an asset such as a brand (e.g. Coca Cola) or a patent, such as Viagra. It can also simply be a result of the industry's cost structure--for example, the large fixed costs that tend to create natural monopolies in utility industries. To be sustainable, the advantage must be:

1. distinctive, and
2. proprietary

In 2006, Jaynie L. Smith authored Creating Competitive Advantage (Doubleday). This book outlines how companies fail to understand their own existing competitive advantages and use them in sales/marketing. She provides a framework for how companies can evaluate their own operations and develop competitive advantage/competitive positioning statements to better hone their sales/marketing messages. Competitive advantage statements help distinguish companies by highlighting what they offer to the customer using tangible terms and concepts. The next step is to test those CA statements through independent market research. This allows a company to understand their customers' hierarchy of buying criteria in an objective indepenedent context. From there, companies can tailor their CA statements to speak directly to the buying interests of the customer.

Competitive Advantage: a company is said to have a competitive advantage over its rivals when its profitability is greater than the average profitability of all other companies competing for the same set of customers.

Sustainable Competitive Advantage: a company has a sustained competitive advantage when its strategies enable it to maintain above-average profitability for a number of years. Competitive advantages vary from situation to situation and from time to time. Some basic examples of CAs can be divided in 4 main global areas:

Cost: Low-cost operations

Quality: High quality, Consistent quality

Time: Delivery speed, On-time delivery, Development speed

Flexibility: Customization, Volume flexibility, Variety

BUSINESS PLANNING

Planning

Planning is both the organizational process of creating and maintaining a plan; and the psychological process of thinking about the activities required to create a desired future on some scale. As such, it is a fundamental property of intelligent behaviour. This thought process is essential to the creation and refinement of a plan, or integration of it with other plans, that is, it combines forecasting of developments with the prepararation of scenarios of how to react to them. The term is also used to describe the formal procedures used in such an endeavor, such as the creation of documents, diagrams, or meetings to discuss the important issues to be addressed, the objectives to be met, and the strategy to be followed. Beyond this, planning has a different meaning depending on the political or economic context in which it is used.

The Planning Process

The planning process provides the framework for developing conservation plans on the basis of ecological, economic, social, and policy considerations. Implementation of these plans may then be facilitated by utilizing technical, educational, and financial assistance programs from NRCS or other sources.

The same planning process is used to develop conservation plans and areawide conservation plans or assessments, but different activities are required to complete each step of the process. Guidance in this handbook is separated accordingly into conservation planning and areawide conservation planning. On-site visits with the client are an integral part of the planning process.

Conservation plans are normally developed with an individual decision-maker. An areawide conservation plan or assessment reflects the desired future conditions developed in conjunction with the client and other stakeholders in the area. The stakeholders may, or more likely may not, be decision-makers for implementing planned activities.

Applications

In Public Policy

Planning refers to the practice and the profession associated with the idea of planning an idea yourself, (land use planning, urban planning or spatial planning). In many countries, the operation of a town and country planning system is often referred to as 'planning' and the professionals which operate the system are known as 'planners'....... Planning: Planning is a process for accomplishing purpose. It is blue print of business growth and a road map of development. It helps in deciding objectives both in quantitative and qualitative terms. It is setting of goals on the basis of objectives and keeping in view the resources.

It is a conscious as well as sub-conscious activity. It is "an anticipatory decision making process " that helps in coping with complexities. It is deciding future course of action from amongst alternatives. It is a process that involves making and evaluating each set of interrelated decisions. It is selection of missions, objectives and " translation of knowledge into action."

A planned performance brings better results compared to unplanned one. A Managers' job is planning, monitoring and controlling. Planning and goal setting are important traits of an organization. It is done at all levels of the organization. Planning includes the plan, the thought process, action, and implementation. Planning gives more power over the future. Planning is deciding in advance what to do, how to do it, when to do it, and who should do it. It bridges the gap from where the organization is to where it wants to be. The planning function involves establishing goals and arranging them in logical order.

Purpose of Plan

Just as no two organizations are alike, so also their plans. It is therefore important to prepare a plan keeping in view the necessities of the enterprise. A plan is important aspect of business. It serves following three critical functions: Helps management to clarify, focus and research their businesses or project's development and prospects. Provides a considered and logical framework within which a business can develop and pursue business strategies over the next three to five years. Offers a benchmark against which actual performance can be measured and reviewed.

How a Plan should be?

A plan should be a realistic view of the expectations. Depending upon the activities, a plan can be Long Range, Intermediate range and of Short range. It the framework within which it must operate. For management seeking external support, the plan is the most important document and key to growth. Preparation of a comprehensive plan will not guarantee success, but lack of a sound plan will, almost certainly, ensures failure.

Importance of the Planning Process

A plan can play a vital role in helping to avoid mistakes or recognize hidden opportunities. Preparing a satisfactory plan of the organization is essential. The planning process enables management to understand more clearly what they want to achieve, and how and when they can do it.

A well-prepared business plan demonstrates that the managers know the business and that they have thought through its development in terms of products, management, finances, and most importantly, markets and competition.

Preparing Plan

Planning is not done off hand. It is prepared after careful and extensive research. For a comprehensive business plan, management has to

- Clearly define the target / goal in writing.
  1. It should be set by person having authority
  2. The goal should be realistic
  3. Specific
  4. Acceptability
  5. Easily measurable
- Identify all the main issues, which need to be addressed.
- Review past performance.
- Decide budgetary requirement
- Focus on matters of strategic importance.
- What are requirements and how will it be met.
- What will be the likely length of the plan and its structure?
- Identify Shortcomings in the concept and gaps.
- Strategies for implementation.
- Review periodically.

In Organizations

Planning is also a management function, concerned with defining goals for future organizational performance and deciding on the tasks and resources to be used in order to attain those goals. To meet the goals, managers may develop plans such as a business plan or a marketing plan. Planning always has a purpose. The purpose may be achievement of certain goals or targets. The planning helps to achieve these goals or target by using the available time and resources. To minimize the timing and resources also require proper planning..

BUSINESS PLAN

Informal or ad-hoc plans are created by individuals in all of their pursuits. Structured and formal plans, used by multiple people, are more likely to occur in projects, diplomacy, careers, economic development, military campaigns, combat, or in the conduct of other business.

It is common for less formal plans to be created as abstract ideas, and remain in that form as they are maintained and put to use. More formal plans as used for business and military purposes, while initially created with and as an abstract thought, are likely to be written down, drawn up or otherwise stored in a form that is accessible to multiple people across time and space. This allows more reliable collaboration in the execution of the plan.

Planning

The term planning implies the working out of sub-components in some degree of detail. Broader-brush enunciations of objectives may qualify as metaphorical roadmaps. Planning literally just means the creation of a plan; it can be as simple as making a list. It has acquired a technical meaning, however, to cover the area of government legislation and regulations related to the use of resources.

Planning can refer to the planned use of any and all resources, as in the succession of Five-Year Plans through which the government of the Soviet Union sought to develop the country. However, the term is most frequently used in relation to planning for the use of land and related resources, for example in urban planning, transportation planning, and so forth. Thus, in a governmental context, "planning" without any qualification is most likely to mean the regulation of land use. See also zoning.

Quotation

Plans are of little importance, but planning is essential-Winston Churchill

Plans are nothing; planning is everything. --Dwight D. Eisenhower

No battleplan survives contact with the enemy.

Methodology

The discipline of planning has occupied great minds and theoreticians. Concepts such as top-down planning (as opposed to bottom-up planning) reveal similarities with the systems thinking behind the Top-Down Model.

The subject touches such broad fields as psychology, game theory, communications and information theory, which inform the planning methods that people seek to use and refine; as well as logic and science (ie methodological naturalism) which serve as a means of testing different parts of a plan for reliability or consistency.

The specific methods used to create and refine plans depends on who is to make it, who is to put it to use, and what resources are available for the task. The methods used by an individual in their mind or personal organiser, may be very different from the collection of planning techniques found in a corporate board-room, and the planning done by a project manager has different priorities and uses different tools to the planning done by an engineer or industrial designer.

Types of Plan

In military usage, the grand structured pre-set plans of World War I became the more flexible and less pretentious limited-objective operations of World War II and later.

Economic planning became an important discipline in the Soviet Union and in Japan--in the West the word "planner" may rather evoke images of town planning.

TIME MANAGEMENT

Time management is commonly defined as the management of time in order to make the most out of it.

But in a 2001 interview, David Allen observed: You can't manage time, it just is. So "time management" is a mislabeled problem, which has little chance of being an effective approach. What you really manage is your activity during time, and defining outcomes and physical actions required is the core process required to manage what you do.

Time management can refer to all of the practices that individuals follow to make better use of their time, but such a definition could range over such diverse areas as the selection and use of personal electronic devices, time and motion study , self-awareness, and indeed a great deal of self-help. As narrowly defined, it refers to principles and systems that individuals use to make conscious decisions about the activities that occupy their time.

Early History

The label "time management" cannot predate the widespread use of the word "management" in our sense at the beginning of the 20th century. Popular self-help books on the subject were published around the same time (Arnold Bennett and Orison Swett). Concerns about the wise use of time have a longer history, reflected in the large number of proverbs concerning time and its utilization, dating at least to Classical Greece and to the Old Testament and other wisdom literature. For many years management texts did not emphasize the personal productivity of the manager.

Many popular management texts had no explicit material on time management or personal productivity management. When it was covered the coverage was brief and often linked with stress management.

Contemporary Time Management

In First Things First, Stephen R. Covey and his co-authors offered a categorization scheme for the hundreds of time management approaches that they reviewed:

- First generation: reminders (based on clocks and watches, but with computer implementation possible) can be used to alert of the time when a task is to be done.
- Second generation: planning and preparation (based on calendar and appointment books) includes setting goals.
- Third generation: planning, prioritizing, controlling (using a personal organizer, other paper-based objects, or computer-or PDA-based systems) activities on a daily basis. This approach implies spending some time in clarifying values and priorities.
- Fourth generation: being efficient and proactive (using any tools above) places goals and roles as the controlling element of the system and favors importance over urgency.

In an alternative classification scheme, the same authors characterize several approaches taken in the time management literature paraphrased as:

- "Get Organized"-paperwork and task triage
- "Protect Your Time"-insolate, isolate, delegate
- "Achieve through Goal Focus"-motivational emphasis
- "Work in Priority Order"-set goals and prioritize

- "Use Magical Tools to Get More Out of Your Time"-depends on when written
- "Master the Skills of Time Management"
- "Go with the Flow"-natural rhythms, Eastern philosophy
- "Recover from Bad Time Habits"-recovery from psychological problems underlying, e.g. procrastination

Overview

Time management strategies are often associated with the recommendation to set goals. These goals are recorded and may be broken down into a project, an action plan, or a simple task list. For individual tasks or for goals, an importance rating may be established, deadlines may be set, and priorities assigned. This process results in a plan with a task list or a schedule or calendar of activities. Authors may recommend a daily, weekly, monthly or other planning periods, usually fixed, but sometimes variable. Different planning periods may be associated with different scope of planning or review. Authors may or may not emphasize reviews of performance against plan. Routine and recurring tasks may or may not be integrated into the time management plan and, if integrated, the integration can be accomplished in various ways.

Task list

A task list (also to-do list) is a list of tasks to be completed, such as chores or steps toward completing a project. It is an inventory tool that serves as an alternative to memory.

Task lists are used in self-management, grocery lists, business management, project management, and software development. It may involve more than one list. When you accomplish one of the items on a task list, you check it off or cross it off. The traditional method is to write these on a piece of paper with a pen or pencil, usually on a note pad or clip-board. Numerous software equivalents are now available, and many popular e-mail clients include task list applications, as do most PDAs. There are also several web-based task list applications, many of which are free.

Task List Organization

Task lists are often tiered. The simplest tiered system includes a general to-do list (or task-holding file) to record all the tasks the person needs to accomplish, and a daily to-do list which is created each day by transferring tasks from the general to-do list.

Task lists are often Prioritized

- An early advocate of "ABC" prioritization was Alan Lakein (See Books below.). In his system "A" items were the most important ("A-1" the most important within that group), "B" next most important, "C" least important.
- A particular method of applying the ABC method assigns "A" to tasks to be done within a day, "B" a week, and "C" a month.
- To prioritize a daily task list, one either records the tasks in the order of highest priority, or assigns them a number after they are listed ("1" for highest priority, "2" for second highest priority, etc.) which indicates in which order to execute the tasks. The latter method is generally faster, allowing the tasks to be recorded more quickly.

Alternatives to Prioritizing

A completely different approach which argues against prioritising altogether was put forward by British author Mark Forster in his book "Do It Tomorrow and Other Secrets of Time Management". This is based on the idea of operating "closed" to-do lists, instead of the traditional "open" to-do list. He argues that the traditional never-ending to-do lists virtually guarantees that some of your work will be left undone. His approach advocates getting all your work done, every day, and if you are unable to achieve it helps you diagnose where you are going wrong and what needs to change.

Software Applications

Modern task list applications may have built-in task hierarchy (tasks are composed of subtasks which again may contain subtasks) , may support multiple methods of filtering and ordering the list of tasks, and may allow to associate arbitrarily long notes for each task.

In contrast to the concept of allowing the person to use multiple filtering methods, at least one new software product additionally contains a mode where the software will attempt to dynamically determine the best tasks for any given moment.

Task list applications may be thought of as lightweight personal information manager or project management software.

Resistors

- Fear of change: Change can be daunting and one may be afraid to change what's proven to work in the past.
- Uncertainty: Even with the change being inevitable, one may be hesitant as being not sure where to start. Uncertainty about when or how to begin making a change can be significant.
- Time pressure: To save time, one has to invest time, and this time investment may be a cause of concern.

Fearing that changing may involve more work at the start--and thus, in the very short term, make things worse--is a common resistor.

- Lack of will power: Why change if one really not need to? The greatest problem is a lack of will.

Drivers

- Increased effectiveness: One may feel the need to make more time so as to be more effective in performing the job and carrying out responsibilities.
- Performance improvement: Time management is an issue that often arises during performance appraisals or review meetings.
- Personal development: One may view changing the approach to time management as a personal development issue and reap the benefit of handling time differently at work and at home.
- Increased responsibilities: A change in time-management approach may become necessary as a result of a promotion or additional responsibilities. Since there is more work to do, and still the same amount of time to do it in, the approach must change.

Caveats

Dwelling on the Lists

- According to Sandberg , task lists "aren't the key to productivity [that] they're cracked up to be". He reports an estimated "30% of listers spend more time managing their lists than [they do] completing what's on them".
- This could be caused by procrastination: by prolonging the planning activity, the individual avoids the tasks he should be doing by creating the illusion that he's still necessarily preparing for them. This is akin to

analysis paralysis. As with any activity, there's a point of diminishing returns. For a task system to be efficient and effective, the user must recognize this, conquer his or her procrastination, and focus on completing the tasks.

Rigid Adherence

- Hendrickson asserts that rigid adherence to task lists can create a "tyranny of the to-do list" that forces one to "waste time on unimportant activities".
- Again, the point of diminishing returns applies here too, but toward the size of the task. Some level of detail must be taken for granted for a task system to work. Rather than put "clean the kitchen", "clean the bedroom", and "clean the bathroom", it is more efficient to put "housekeeping" and save time spent writing and reduce the system's administrative load (each task entered into the system generates a cost in time and effort to manage it, aside from the execution of the task). The risk of consolidating tasks, however, is that "housekeeping" in this example may prove overwhelming or nebulously defined, which will either increase the risk of procrastination, or a mismanaged project.
- Listing routine tasks wastes time. If you are in the habit of brushing your teeth every day, then there is no reason to put it down on the task list. The same goes for getting out of bed, fixing meals, etc. If you need to track routine tasks, then a standard list or chart may be useful, to avoid the procedure of manually listing these items over and over.
- To remain flexible, a task system must allow adaptation, in the form of rescheduling in the face of unexpected problems and opportunities, to save time spent on irrelevant or less than optimal tasks.

- To avoid getting stuck in a wasteful pattern, the task system should also include regular (monthly, semi-annual, and annual) planning and system-evaluation sessions, to weed out inefficiencies and ensure the user is headed in the direction he or she truly desires.
- If some time is not regularly spent on achieving long-range goals, the individual may get stuck in a perpetual holding pattern on short-term plans, like staying at a particular job much longer than originally planned.

Set goals for oneself and work on achieving these goals. Some people study in different ways so you are to find out how you are able to study and put that into action. Some people are able to understand their work if they can see it. Some need to touch and feel whatever is being spoken about in the book. Some people need to see what they are studying in order to understand what is coming out of the book.

Techniques for Setting Priorities

ABC Analysis

A technique that has been used in business management for a long time is the categorization of large data into groups. These groups are often marked A, B, and C-hence the name. Activities that are perceived as having highest priority are assigned an A, those with lowest priority are labeled C. ABC analysis can incorporate more than three groups. ABC analysis is frequently combined with Pareto analysis.

Pareto Analysis

This is the idea that 80% of tasks can be completed in 20% of the disposable time. The remaining 20% of tasks will take up 80% of the time. This principle is used to sort tasks into two parts. According to this form of Pareto analysis it is recommended that tasks that fall into the first category be assigned a higher priority.

The 80-20-rule can also be applied to increase productivity: it is assumed that 80% of the productivity can be achieved by doing 20% of the tasks. If productivity is the aim of time management, then these tasks should be prioritized higher.

Fit

Essentially, fit is the congruence of the requirements of a task (location, financial investment, time, etc.) with the available resources at the time. Often people are constrained by externally controlled schedules, locations, etc., and "fit" allows us to maximize our productivity given those constraints. For example, if one encounters a gap of 15 minutes in their schedule, it is typically more efficient to complete a task that would require 15 minutes, than to complete a task that can be done in 5 minutes, or to start a task that would take 4 weeks. This concept also applies to time of the day: free time at 7am is probably less usefully applied to the goal of learning the drums, and more productively a time to read a book. Lastly, fit can be applied to location: free time at home would be used differently from free time at work, in town, etc.

Posec Method

POSEC is an acronym for Prioritize by Organizing, Streamlining, Economizing and Contributing.

The method dictates a template which emphasises an average individual's immediate sense of emotional and monetary security. It suggests that by attending to one's personal responsibilities first, an individual is better positioned to shoulder collective responsibilities. Inherent in the acronym is a hierarchy of self-realization which mirrors Abraham Maslow's "Hierarchy of needs".

1. PRIORITIZE-Your time and define your life by goals.
2. ORGANIZING-Things you have to accomplish regularly to be successful. (Family and Finances)
3. STREAMLINING-Things you may not like to do, but must do. (Work and Chores)
4. ECONOMIZING-Things you should do or may even like to do, but they're not pressingly urgent. (Pasttimes and Socializing)
5. CONTRIBUTING-By paying attention to the few remaining things that make a difference. (Social Obligations)

The Eisenhower Method

All tasks are evaluated using the criteria important/ unimportant and urgent/not urgent and put in according quadrants. Tasks in unimportant/not urgent are dropped, tasks in important/urgent are done immediately and personally, tasks in unimportant/urgent are delegated and tasks in important/not urgent get an end date and are done personally. This method is said to have been used by US President Dwight D. Eisenhower, and is outlined in a quote attributed to him: What is important is seldom urgent and what is urgent is seldom important.

AUTOMATED PLANNING AND SCHEDULING

Automated planning and scheduling is a branch of artificial intelligence that concerns the realisation of strategies or action sequences, typically for execution by intelligent agents, autonomous robots and unmanned vehicles. Unlike classical control and classification problems, the solutions are complex, unknown and have to be discovered and optimised in multidimensional space. In known environments with available models planning can be done offline. Solutions can be found and evaluated prior to execution. In dynamically unknown environments the strategy often needs to be revised online. Models and policies need to be adapted. Solutions usually resort to iterative trial and error processes commonly seen in artificial intelligence. These include dynamic programming, reinforcement learning and combinatorial optimization.

A typical planner takes three inputs: a description of the initial state of the world, a description of the desired goal, and a set of possible actions, all encoded in a formal language such as STRIPS. The planner produces a sequence of actions that lead from the initial state to a state meeting the goal. An alternative language for describing planning problems is that of hierarchical task networks, in which a set of tasks is given, and each task can be either realized by a primitive action or decomposed in a set of other tasks.

The difficulty of planning is dependent on the simplifying assumptions employed, e.g. atomic time, deterministic time, complete observability, etc. Classical planners make all these assumptions and have been studied most fully. Some popular techniques include: forward chaining and backward chaining state-space search, possibly enhanced by the use of relationships among conditions (see graphplan) or heuristics synthesized from the problem, search through plan space, and translation to propositional satisfiability (satplan).

If the assumption of determinism is dropped and a probabilistic model of uncertainty is adopted, then this leads to the problem of policy generation for a Markov decision process (MDP) or (in the general case) Partially observable Markov decision process (POMDP).

ORGANIZING

Organizing is the act of rearranging elements following one or more rules. It can also be seen as the opposite of messing up. One organized opposite could be disordered, since ordered is almost synonymous. The difference between ordered and organized is that something is only ordered as long as it is both organized and standardized.

Examples

Anything is commonly considered organized when it looks like everything has a correct order of placement. But it's only ultimately organized if any element has no difference on time taken to find it. In that sense, organizing can also be defined as to place different objects in logical arrangement for better searching.

Organizations are groups of people frequently trying to organize some specific subject, such as political issues. So, even while organizing can be viewed as a simple definition, it can get as complex as organizing the world's information.

History

Historically, humans have always tried to organize ourselves. Be it on religion, through books and spoken word, or in science, through journals and studies, or in many other ways. Writing ideas in a book, not to talk to someone, but to specifically catalog is also an attempt to organize information. Science books are notable by their organization attempt of a specific subject. Encyclopedias, instead, usually try to organize any subject into one place, for faster indexing and seeking of meanings.

Applications

Organizing, in companies point of view, is the management function that usually follows after planning. And it involves the assignment of tasks, the grouping of tasks into departments and the assignment of authority and allocation of resources across the organization.

Structure

The framework in which the organisation defines how tasks are divided, resources are deployed, and departments are coordinated.

1. A set of formal tasks assigned to individuals and departments.
2. Formal reporting relationships, including lines of authority, decision responsibility, number of hierarchical levels and span of managers control.
3. The design of systems to ensure effective coordination of employees across departments.

Work Specialization

- The degree to which organizational tasks are sub divided into individual jobs; also called division of labour
- With too much specialization, employees are isolated and do only a single, tiny, boring job.
- Many organizations enlarge jobs to provide greater challenges or assigning to tasks that are rotated.

Chain of Command

- An unbroken line of authority that links all individuals in the organisation and specifies who reports to whom.

— Unity of Command-one employee is held accountable to only one supervisor

— Scalar principle-clearly defined line of authority in the organisation that includes all employees

Authority, Responsibility, and Accountability

- Authority-formal and legitimate right of a manager to make decisions, issue orders, and allocate resources to achieve organisationally desired outcomes.

- Responsibility-duty to perform the task or activity an employee has been assigned
- Accountability-the fact that the people with authority and responsibility are subject to reporting and justifying task outcomes to those above them in the chain of command

Delegation

- The process managers use to transfer authority and responsibility to positions below them in the hierarchy
- Organisations today tend to encourage delegation from highest to lowest possible levels
- Can improve flexibility to meet customers needs and adaptation to competitive environments
- Managers often find delegation difficults

Line and Staff Authority

- Line authority-in which individuals in management positions have the formal power to direct and control immediate subordinates.
- Staff authority-granted to staff specialists in their areas of expertise. Narrrower than line authority and includes the right to advise, recommend, and counsel in the staff specialists' area of expertise. It is a communication relationship with management.

Span of Management

Factors influencing larger span of management.

1. Work performed by subordinates is stable and routine.
2. Subordinates perform similar work tasks.
3. Subordinates are concentrated in a single location.
4. Subordinates are highly trained and need little direction in performing tasks.

5. Rules and procedures defining task activities are available.
6. Support systems and personnel are available for the managers.
7. Little time is required in nonsupervisory activities such as coordination with other departments or planning.
8. Managers' personal preferences and styles favour a large span.

Tall vs. Flat Structure

- Tall-A management structure characterised by an overall narrow span of management and a relatively large number of hirarchical levels. Tight control.
- Flat-A management structure characterised by a wide span of control and relatively few hirarchical levels. Loose control. Facilitates delegation.

Centralisation, Decentralisation, and Formalisation

- Centralisation-The location of decision making authority near top organisational levels.
- Decentralisation-The location of decision making authority near lower organisational levels.
- Formalisation-The written documentation used to direct and control employees.

Departmentalization

The basis on which individuals are grouped into departments and departments into total organisations.

Approach options include;

1. Functional-by common skills and work tasks
2. Divisional-common product, programme or geographical location

3. Matrix-combination of Functional and Divisional
4. Team-to accompllish specific tasks
5. Network-departments are independent providing functions for a central core breaker

Importance of Organising

- Organisations are often troubled by how to organise, particularly when a new strategy is developed
- Changing market conditions or new technology requires change
- Organisations seek efficiencies through improvements in organizing.

ORDER THEORY

Order theory is a branch of mathematics that studies various kinds of binary relations that capture the intuitive notion of a mathematical ordering. This article gives a detailed introduction to the field and includes some of the most basic definitions. For a quick lookup of order-theoretic terms, there is also an order theory glossary. A list of order topics collects the various articles in the vicinity of order theory.

Background and Motivation

Orders appear everywhere-at least as far as mathematics and related areas, such as computer science, are concerned. The first order that one typically meets in primary school mathematical education is the order ? of natural numbers. This intuitive concept is easily extended to orderings of other sets of numbers, such as the integers and the reals. Indeed the idea of being greater or smaller than another number is one of the basic intuitions of number systems in general (although one usually is also interested in the actual difference of two numbers, which is not given by the order).

Another familiar example of an ordering is the lexicographic order of words in a dictionary.

The above types of orders have a special property: each element can be compared to any other element, i.e. it is either greater, smaller, or equal. However, this is not always a desired requirement.

For example, consider the subset ordering of sets. If a set A contains all the elements of a set B, then B is said to be smaller than or equal to A. Yet there are some sets that cannot be related in this fashion. Whenever both contain some elements that are not in the other, the two sets are not related by subset-inclusion. Hence, subset-inclusion is only a partial order, as opposed to the total orders given before.

Order theory captures the intuition of orders that arises from such examples in a general setting. This is achieved by specifying properties that a relation ? must have to be a mathematical order. This more abstract approach makes much sense, because one can derive numerous theorems in the general setting, without focusing on the details of any particular order. These insights can then be readily transferred to many concrete applications.

Driven by the wide practical usage of orders, numerous special kinds of ordered sets have been defined, some of which have grown to mathematical fields of their own. In addition, order theory does not restrict itself to the various classes of ordering relations, but also considers appropriate functions between them. A simple example of an order theoretic property for functions comes from analysis where monotone functions are found frequently.

Basic Definitions

This section introduces ordered sets by building upon the concepts of set theory, arithmetics, and binary relations.

Partially Ordered Sets

Orders are special binary relations. Suppose that P is a set and that ≤ is a relation on P. Then ≤ is a partial order if it is reflexive, antisymmetric, and transitive, i.e., for all a, b and c in P, we have that:

a ≤ a (reflexivity)

if a ≤ b and b ≤ a then a = b (antisymmetry)

if a ≤ b and b ≤ c then a ≤ c (transitivity)

A set with a partial order on it is called a partially ordered set, poset, or just an ordered set if the intended meaning is clear. By checking these properties, one immediately sees that the well-known orders on natural numbers, integers, rational numbers and reals are all orders in the above sense. However, they have the additional property of being total, i.e., for all a and b in P, we have that:

a ≤ b or b ≤ a (totality)

These orders can also be called linear orders or chains. While many classical orders are linear, the subset order on sets provides an example where this is not the case. Another example is given by the divisibility relation "|". For two natural numbers n and m, we write n|m if n divides m without remainder. One easily sees that this yields a partial order. The identity relation = on any set is also a partial order in which every two elements are incomparable. It is also the only relation that is both a partial order and an equivalence relation. Many advanced properties of posets are mainly interesting for non-linear orders.

Visualizing a Poset

Hasse diagrams can visually represent the elements and relations of a partial ordering. These are graph drawings where the vertices are the elements of the poset and the ordering relation is indicated by both the edges and the relative positioning of the vertices. Orders are drawn bottom-up: if an element x is smaller than (preceeds) y then there exists a path from x to y that is directed upwards. It is often necessary for the edges connecting elements to cross each other, but elements must never be located within an edge. An instructive exercise is to draw the Hasse diagram for the set of natural numbers that are smaller than or equal to 13, ordered by | (the divides relation).

Even some infinite sets can be diagrammed by superimposing an ellipsis (...) on a finite sub-order. This works well for the natural numbers, but it fails for the reals, where there is no immediate successor above 0. However, quite often one can obtain an intuition related to diagrams of a similar kind.

Special Elements within an Order

In a partially ordered set there may be some elements that play a special rol The most basic example is given by the least element of a poset. For example, 1 is the least element of the positive integers and the empty set is the least set under the subset order. Formally, an element m is a least element if:

m ≤ a, for all elements a of the order.

The notation 0 is frequently found for the least element, even when no numbers are concerned. However, in orders on sets of numbers, this notation might be inappropriate or ambiguous, since the number 0 is not always least. An example is given by the above divisibility order |, where 1 is the least element since it divides all other numbers. On the other hand, 0 is the number that is divided by all other numbers. Hence it is the greatest element of the order. Other frequent terms for the least and greatest elements is bottom and top or zero and unit. Least and greatest elements may fail to exist, as the example of the real numbers shows.

On the other hand, if they exist, least and greatest elements are always unique. In contrast, consider the divisibility relation | on the set {2,3,4,5,6}. Although this set has neither top nor bottom, the elements 2, 3, and 5 do not have any elements below them, while 4, 5, and 6 have no other number above. Such elements are called minimal and maximal, respectively. Formally, an element m is minimal if:

a ≤ m implies a = m, for all elements a of the order.

Exchanging ? with ? yields the definition of maximality. As the example shows, there can be many maximal elements and some elements may be both maximal and minimal (e.g. 5 above). However, if there is a least element, then it is the only minimal element of the order. Again, in infinite posets maximal elements do not always exist-the set of all finite subsets of a given infinite set, ordered by subset inclusion, provides one out of many counterexamples. An important tool to ensure the existence of maximal elements under certain conditions is Zorn's Lemma.

Subsets of partially ordered sets inherit the order. We already applied this by considering the subset {2,3,4,5,6} of the natural numbers with the induced divisibility ordering. Now there are also elements of a poset that are special with respect to some subset of the order. This leads to the definition of upper bounds. Given a subset S of some poset P, an upper bound of S is an element b of P that is above all elements of S. Formally, this means that

s ≤ b, for all s in S.

Lower bounds again are defined by inverting the order. For example,-5 is a lower bound of the natural numbers as a subset of the integers. Given a set of sets, an upper bound for these sets under the subset ordering is given by their union. In fact, this upper bound is quite special: it is the smallest set that contains all of the sets. Hence, we have found the least upper bound of a set of sets. This concept is also called supremum or join, and for a set S one writes sup(S) or vS for its least upper bound. Conversely, the greatest lower bound is known as infimum or meet and denoted inf(S) or ^S. These concepts play an important role in many applications of order theory. For two elements x and y, one also writes x v y and x ^ y for sup({x,y}) and inf({x,y}), respectively. (Using Wikipedia's TeX markup, one can also write and, as well as the larger symbols v and ^. Note however, that all of these symbols may fail to match the font size of the standard text and should therefore preferably be used in extra lines. The rendering of for v and for ^ is not supported by many of today's web browsers across all platforms and therefore avoided here.)

For another example, consider again the relation | on natural numbers. The least upper bound of two numbers is the smallest number that is divided by both of them, i.e. the least common multiple of the numbers. Greatest lower bounds in turn are given by the greatest common divisor.

Duality

In the previous definitions, we often noted that a concept can be defined by just inverting the ordering in a former definition. This is the case for "least" and "greatest", for "minimal" and "maximal", for "upper bound" and "lower bound", and so on. This is a general situation in order theory: A given order can be inverted by just exchanging its direction, pictorially flipping the Hasse diagram top-down. This yields the so-called dual, inverse, or opposite order.

Every order theoretic definition has its dual: it is the notion one obtains by applying the definition to the inverse order. Since the symmetry of all concepts, this operation preserves the theorems of partial orders. For a given mathematical result, one can just invert the order and replace all definitions by their duals and one obtains another valid theorem. This is important and useful, since one obtains two theorems for the price of one. Some more details and examples can be found in the article on duality in order theory.

Constructing new Orders

There are many ways to construct orders out of given orders. The dual order is one example. Another important construction is the cartesian product of two partially ordered sets, taken together with the product order on pairs of elements. The ordering is defined by (a, x) ≤ (b, y) if (and only if) a ≤ b and x ≤ y. (Notice carefully that there are three distinct meanings for the relation symbol ≤ in this definition.) The disjoint union of two posets is another typical example of order construction, where the order is just the (disjoint) union of the original orders.

Every partial order ≤ gives rise to a so-called strict order ≤, by defining a < b if a ≤ b and not b ≤ a. This transformation can be inverted by setting a ≤ b if a < b or a = b. The two concepts are equivalent although in some circumstances one can be more convenient to work with than the other.

Functions between Orders

It is reasonable to consider functions between partially ordered sets having certain additional properties, that are related to the ordering relations of the two sets. The most fundamental condition that occurs in this context is monotonicity. A function f from a poset P to a poset Q is monotone, or order-preserving, if a ≤ b in P implies f(a) ≤ f(b) in Q (Noting that, strictly, the two relations here are different since they apply to different sets.). The converse of this implication leads to functions that are order-reflecting, i.e. functions f as above for which f(a) ≤ f(b) implies a ≤ b. On the other hand, a function may also be order-reversing or antitone, if a ≤ b implies f(b) ≤ f(a).

An order-embedding is a function f between orders that is both order-preserving and order-reflecting. Examples for these definitions are found easily. For instance, the function that maps a natural number to its successor is clearly monotone with respect to the natural order. Any function from a discrete order, i.e. from a set ordered by the identity order "=", is also monotone. Mapping each natural number to the corresponding real number gives an example for an order embedding. The set complement on a powerset is an example of an antitone function.

An important question is when two orders are "essentially equal", i.e. when they are the same up to renaming of elements. Order isomorphisms are functions that define such a renaming. An order-isomorphism is a monotone bijective function that has a monotone inverse. This is equivalent to being a surjective order-embedding. Hence, the image f(P) of an order-embedding is always isomorphic to P, which justifies the term "embedding".

A more elaborate type of functions is given by so-called Galois connections. Monotone Galois connections can be viewed as a generalization of order-isomorphisms, since they constitute of a pair of two functions in converse directions, which are "not quite" inverse to each other, but that still have close relationships.

Another special type of self-maps on a poset are closure operators, which are not only monotonic, but also idempotent, i.e. f(x) = f(f(x)), and extensive (or inflationary), i.e. x ≤ f(x). These have many applications in all kinds of "closures" that appear in mathematics. Besides being compatible with the mere order relations, functions between posets may also behave well with respect to special elements and constructions. For example, when talking about posets with least element, it may seem reasonable to consider only monotonic functions that preserve this element, i.e. which map least elements to least elements. If binary infima ^ exist, then a reasonable property might be to require that f(x ^ y) = f(x) ⊥(y), for all x and y. All of these properties, and indeed many more, may be compiled under the label of limit-preserving functions.

Finally, one can invert the view, switching from functions of orders to orders of functions. Indeed, the functions between two posets P and Q can be ordered via the pointwise order. For two functions f and g, we have f ≤ g if f(x) ≤ g(x) for all elements x of P. This occurs for example in domain theory, where function spaces play an important role.

Special Types of Orders

Many of the structures that are studied in order theory employ order relations with further properties. In fact, even some relations that are not partial orders are of special interest. Mainly the concept of a preorder has to be mentioned. A preorder is a relation that is reflexive and transitive, but not necessarily antisymmetric. Each preorder induces an equivalence relation between elements, where a is equivalent to b, if a ? b and b ? a. Preorders can be turned into orders by identifying all elements that are equivalent with respect to this relation.

Basic types of special orders have already been given in form of total orders. An additional simple but useful property leads to so-called well-orders, for which all non-empty subsets have a minimal element. Generalizing well-orders from linear to partial orders, a set is well partially ordered if all its non-empty subsets have a finite number of minimal elements.

Many other types of orders arise when the existence of infima and suprema of certain sets is guaranteed. Focusing on this aspect, usually referred to as completeness of orders, one obtains:

- Bounded posets, i.e. posets with a least and greatest element (which are just the supremum and infimum of the empty subset),
- Lattices, in which every non-empty finite set has a supremum and infimum,
- Complete lattices, where every set has a supremum and infimum, and
- Directed complete partial orders (dcpos), that guarantee the existence of suprema of all directed subsets and that are studied in domain theory.

However, one can go even further: if all finite non-empty infima exist, then ^ can be viewed as a total binary operation in the sense of universal algebra. Hence, in a lattice, two operations ^ and v are available, and one can define new properties by giving identities, such as

x ^ (y v z) = (x ^ y) v (x ^ z), for all x, y, and z.

This condition is called distributivity and gives rise to distributive lattices. There are some other important distributivity laws which are discussed in the article on distributivity in order theory. Some additional order structures that are often specified via algebraic operations and defining identities are

- Heyting algebras and
- Boolean algebras,

which both introduce a new operation ~ called negation. Both structures play a role in mathematical logic and especially Boolean algebras have major applications in computer science. Finally, various structures in mathematics combine orders with even more algebraic operations, as in the case of quantales, that allow for the definition of an addition operation.

Many other important properties of posets exist. For example, a poset is locally finite if every closed interval [a, b] in it is finite. Locally finite posets give rise to incidence algebras which in turn can be used to define the Euler characteristic of finite bounded posets.

Subsets of Ordered Sets

In an ordered set, one can define many types of special subsets based on the given order. A simple example are upper sets; i.e. sets that contain all elements that are above them in the order. Formally, the upper closure of a set S in a poset P is given by the set {x in P | there is some y in S with y ≤ x}. A set that is equal to its upper closure is called an upper set. Lower sets are defined dually.

More complicated lower subsets are ideals, which have the additional property that each two of their elements have an upper bound within the ideal. Their duals are given by filters. A related concept is that of a directed subset, which like an ideal contains upper bounds of finite subsets, but does not have to be a lower set. Furthermore it is often generalized to preordered sets. A subset which is-as a sub-poset-linearly ordered, is called a chain. The opposite notion, the antichain, is a subset that contains no two comparable elements; i.e. that is a discrete order.

Related Mathematical Areas

Although most mathematical areas use orders in one or the other way, there are also a few theories that have relationships which go far beyond mere application. Together with their major touching points with order theory, some of these are to be presented below.

Universal Algebra

As already mentioned, the methods and formalisms of universal algebra are an important tool for many order theoretic considerations. Beside formalizing orders in terms of algebraic structures that satisfy certain identities, one can also establish other connections to algebra. An example is given by the correspondence between Boolean algebras and Boolean rings. Other issues are concerned with the existence of free constructions, such as free lattices based on a given set of generators. Furthermore, closure operators are important in the study of universal algebra.

Topology

In topology orders play a very prominent role. In fact, the set of open sets provides a classical example of a complete lattice, more precisely a complete Heyting algebra (or "frame" or "locale"). Filters and nets are notions closely related to order theory and the closure operator of sets can be used to define topology. Beyond these relations, topology can be looked at solely in terms of the open set lattices, which leads to the study of pointless topology. Furthermore, a natural preorder of elements of the underlying set of a topology is given by the so-called specialization order, that is actually a partial order if the topology is T_0.

Conversely, in order theory, one often makes use of topological results. There are various ways to define subsets of an order which can be considered as open sets of a topology. Especially, it is interesting to consider topologies on a poset (X, ≤) that in turn induce ≤ as their specialization order. The finest such topology is the Alexandrov topology, given by taking all upper sets as opens. Conversely, the coarsest topology that induces the specialization order is the upper topology, having the complements of principal ideals (i.e. sets of the form {y in X | y ≤ x} for some x) as a subbase. Additionally, a topology with specialization order?

may be order consistent, meaning that their open sets are "inaccessible by directed suprema" (with respect to ≤). The finest order consistent topology is the Scott topology, which is coarser than the Alexandrov topology. A third important topology in this spirit is the Lawson topology. There are close connections between these topologies and the concepts of order theory. For example, a function preserves directed suprema iff it is continuous with respect to the Scott topology (for this reason this order theoretic property is also called Scott-continuity).

Category Theory

The visualization of orders with Hasse diagrams has a straightforward generalization: instead of displaying lesser elements below greater ones, the direction of the order can also be depicted by giving directions to the edges of a graph. In this way, each order is seen to be equivalent to a directed acyclic graph, where the nodes are the elements of the poset and there is a directed path from a to b if and only if a ≤ b. Dropping the requirement of being acyclic, one can also obtain all preorders.

When equipped with all transitive edges, these graphs in turn are just special categories, where elements are objects and each set of morphisms between two elements is at most singleton. Functions between orders become functors between categories. Interestingly, many ideas of order theory are just concepts of category theory in small. For example, an infimum is just a categorical product. More generally, one can capture suprema and infima under the abstract notion of a categorical limit (or colimit, respectively). Another place where categorical ideas occur is the concept of a (monotone) Galois connection, which is just the same as a pair of adjoint functors.

But category theory also has its impact on order theory on a larger scale. Classes of posets with appropriate functions as discussed above form interesting categories. Often one can also state constructions of orders, like the product order, in terms of categories. Further insights result when categories of orders are found categorically equivalent to other categories, for example of topological spaces. This line of research leads to various representation theorems, often collected under the label of Stone duality.

History

As explained before, orders are ubiquitous in mathematics. However, earliest explicit mentionings of partial orders are probably to be found not before the 19th century. In this context the works of George Boole are of great importance. Moreover, works of Charles S. Peirce, Richard Dedekind, and Ernst Schröder also consider concepts of order theory. Certainly, there are others to be named in this context and surely there exists more detailed material on the history of order theory. Please contribute if any further knowledge is available to you. The term poset as an abbreviation for partially ordered set was coined by Garrett Birkhoff in the second edition of his influential book Lattice Theory.

SORTING

Sorting is any process of arranging items in some sequence and/or in different sets, and accordingly, it has two common, yet distinct meanings:

1. ordering: arranging items of the same kind, class, nature, etc. in some ordered sequence,
2. categorizing: grouping and labelling items with similar properties together (by sorts).

Sorting Information or Data

For sorting we can either specify a weak order "should not come after" or a strict weak order "should come before" (specifying one defines also the other, the two are the complement of the inverse of each other, see operations on binary relations). For the sorting to be unique, these two are restricted to a total order and a strict total order, respectively.

Sorting n-tuples (depending on context also called e.g. records consisting of fields) can be done based on one or more of its components. More generally objects can be sorted based on a property. Such a component or property is called a sort key.

For example, the items are books, the sort key is the title, subject or author, and the order is alphabetical.

A new sort key can be created from two or more sort keys by lexicographical order. The first is then called the primary sort key, the second the secondary sort key, etc.

For example, addresses could be sorted using the city as primary sort key, and the street as secondary sort key.

If the sort key values are totally ordered, the sort key defines a weak order of the items: items with the same sort key are equivalent with respect to sorting. See also stable sorting. If different items have different sort key values then this defines a unique order of the items.

A standard order is often called ascending (corresponding to the fact that the standard order of numbers is ascending, i.e. A to Z, 0 to 9), the reverse order descending (Z to A, 9 to 0).

Now if you sort on different keys, then you get different lists of header information (such as the author's name) with the appended tailing records (such as title or publisher). Sorting in computer science is one of the most extensively researched subjects because of the need to speed up the operation on thousands or millions of records during a search operation; see sorting algorithm.

The main purpose of sorting information is to optimise its usefulness for specific tasks. In general, there are two ways of grouping information: by category e.g. a shopping catalogue where items are compiled together under headings such as 'home', 'sport & leisure', 'women's clothes' etc. (nominal scale) and by the intensity of some property, such as price, e.g. from the cheapest to most expensive (ordinal scale). This is illustrated by the following story:

Managers are on a course of basic computer terms and they are explained the meaning of sorting. The lecturer comes in and throws hundreds of various nails and screws, new, old, rusty and crooked, of different size and material on the table. S/he then tells them to: sort! The students in no time create a dozen or so heaps each with relatively homogeneous members, and with some undecided cases left. The lecturer picks up a straight and strong nail, and hammers it in the wall with his/her shoe sole. "You failed to ask sort what for, or what to sort on"-s/he would tell the puzzled audience.

In the book Information Anxiety by Richard Saul Wurman, he proposes that the most common sorting purposes are Name, by Location and by Time (these are actually special cases of category and hierarchy). Together these give the acronym LATCH (Location, Alphabetical, Time, Category, Hierarchy) and can be used to describe just about every type of ordered information.

Often information is sorted using different methods at different levels of abstraction: e.g. the UK telephone directories which are sorted by location, by category (business or residential) and then alphabetically. New media still subscribe to these basic sorting methods: e.g. a Google search returns a list of web pages in a hierarchical list based on its own scoring system for how closely they match the search criteria (from closest match downwards).

The opposite of sorting, rearranging a sequence of items in a random or meaningless order, is called reshuffling.

Physical Sorting Processes

Various sorting tasks are essential in industrial processes. For example, during the extraction of gold from ore, a device called a shaker table uses gravity, vibration, and flow to separate gold from lighter materials in the ore (sorting by size and weight). Sorting is also a naturally occurring process that results in the concentration of ore or sediment. Sorting results from the application of some criterion or differential stressor to a mass to separate it into its components based on some variable quality. Materials that are different, but only slightly so, such as the isotopes of uranium, are very difficult to separate.

COMMUNITY ORGANIZING

Community organizing is a process by which people are brought together to act in common self-interest. While organizing describes any activity involving people interacting with one another in a formal manner, much community organizing is in the pursuit of a common agenda. Many groups seek populist goals and the ideal of participatory democracy. Community organizers create social movements by building a base of concerned people, mobilizing these community members to act, and developing leadership from and relationships among the people involved.

Common Aspects of Organized Communities

Organized community groups seek accountability from elected officials, corporations and institutions as well as increased direct representation within decision-making bodies and social reform. Where negotiations fail, these organizations seek to inform others outside of the organization of the issues being addressed and expose or pressure the decision-makers through a variety of means, including picketing, boycotting, sit-ins, petitioning, and electoral politics.

Community organizing is usually focused on more than just resolving specific issues. Organizing is empowering all community members, often with the end goal of distributing power equally throughout the community.

Community organizers generally seek to build groups that are democratic in governance, open and accessible to community members, and concerned with the general health of the community rather than a specific interest group.

There are three basic types of community organizing, grassroots organizing, faith based community organizing, and coalition building. Additionally, political campaigns often claim that their door-to-door operations are in fact an effort to organize the community, often these operations are focused exclusively on voter identification and turn out.

The ideal of grassroots organizing is to build community groups from scratch, develop new leadership where none existed, and otherwise organize the unorganized. It is a values based process where people are brought together to act in the interest of their communities and the common good. It is a strategy that revitalizes communities and allows the individuals to participate and incite social change. It empowers the people directly involved and impacted by the issues being addressed. A network of community organizations that employ this method is National Peoples Action

Faith-based community organizing, FBCO, is a deliberate methodology of developing the power and relationships throughout a community of institutions such as congregations, unions, and associations. Built on the work of Saul Alinsky in the mid-1900s, there are now 180 FBCOs in the US as well as in South Africa, England,

Germany, and other nations (according to Interfaith Funders' 2001 study Faith Based Community Organizing: State of the Field, by Mark Warren and Richard Wood). Local organizations are often linked through organizing networks such as the Industrial Areas Foundation (IAF), Direct Action and Research Training (DART) Center, and People Improving Communities through Organizing (PICO). For more information view two videos The Power of New Voices and Faith in Action-The PICO Organizing Model.

Coalition building efforts seek instead to unite existing groups, such as churches, civic associations, and social clubs, to more effectively pursue a common agenda.

Community organizing is not solely the domain of progressive politics, as dozens of fundamentalist organizations have sprung up, such as the Christian Coalition.

History of Community Organizing in the United States

Robert Fisher and Peter Romanofsky have grouped the history of community organizing in the United States into four rough periods:

1880 to 1900

People sought to meet the pressures of rapid immigration and industrialization by organizing immigrant neighborhoods in urban centers. Since the emphasis of the reformers was mostly on building community through settlement houses and other service mechanisms, the dominant approach was what Fisher calls social work. During this period The Newsboys Strike provided an early model of youth-led organizing.

1900 to 1940

Community organization was established distinct from social work, with much energy coming from those critical of capitalist doctrines. Studs Terkel documented community organizing in the depression era, perhaps most notably that of Dorothy Day. Most organizations had a national orientation because the economic problems the nation faced did not seem possible to change at the neighborhood levels.

1940 to 1960

The emergence of the distinctive approach of Saul Alinsky spurred new thought and new blood into community movements. Those influenced by Alinsky were (and still are) concerned with social justice without having socialist thought as their primary framework. Alinsky promoted greater awareness of community organizing in academic circles, and those affiliated with Alinsky trained a generation of organizers, including César Chávez.

1960 to present

The American Civil Rights Movement, the anti-war movements, the Chicano movement, the feminist movement, and the gay rights movement all influenced and were influenced by ideas of neighborhood organizing. Experience with federal anti-poverty programs and the upheavals in the cities produced a thoughtful response among activists and theorists in the early 1970s that has informed activities, organizations, strategies and movements through the end of the century. Less dramatically, civic associations and neighborhood block clubs were formed all across the country to foster community spirit and civic duty, as well as provide a social outlet.

Many of the most notable leaders in community organizing today emerged from the National Welfare Rights Organization. John Calkins of DART, Ernesto Cortes of the Industrial Areas Foundation, Wade Rathke of ACORN, John Dodds of Philadelphia Unemployment Project and Mark Splain of the AFL-CIO, among others.

Careers and Training in Community Organizing

A career as a community organizer can be a great option for people who want to make a difference, are concerned about social inequities, and are interested in community solutions and empowering people. People come to careers in community organizing from diverse professions and backgrounds. Many people discover community organizing through participation in some sort of organizing or activist effort in their own communities, and only afterward discover that there are actually jobs and a profession in community organizing. There are graduate and undergraduate programs which focus on community organizing at several colleges and universities in the U.S., such as the University of Maryland--see and, and the University of Vermont.

Some feel that the community organizing field currently is in need of more effective recruitment and training of potential community organizers. They argue that the current situation, which relies primarily on word-of-mouth and some academic programs, is not adequate to meet the need for community organizers. For example, Joe Szakos, in his paper published on the COMM-ORG website, argues that a collective recruitment plan for community organizers is needed.

Several good community organizing training programs exist for people new to the field. These include the DART Organizers Institute, and the Midwest Academy's Internship program. However many of these programs accept only a small number of applicants. For example, the Midwest Academy states that it hires "10 or more community organizing interns." DART says on its website that in 2006 it received "over 1,100 resumes and interviewed over 500 candidates, and finally selected 20 Organizer Trainees." The Industrial Areas Foundation (IAF) also offers summer internships for college students and paid "90-Day Try Outs" at their affiliate organizations. This page on the Center for Community Change websitehas a good list of community organizer training and internship opportunities, with descriptions of each opportunity.

The three training programs mentioned above are paid internship programs. There are also training programs that require participants to pay for the cost of the training, which usually lasts for several days. The Midwest Academy offers such a program. These trainings tend to be geared toward people already involved in community organizing in one way or another, including community leaders (the local people who are constituents of a community organization and lead the efforts).

There are several good resources online with advice and information for people exploring a career in community organizing. These include an info-packed Organizing Guide in the Career Center at idealist.org. Additionally, the COMM-ORG website has a "...How to get Started in Community Organizing" page with info provided by people on their list-serv.

LEADERSHIP

The word leadership can refer to:

1. The process of leading.
2. Those entities that perform one or more acts of leading.
3. The ability to affect human behavior so as to accomplish a mission designated by the leader

Terminology, Usage and Conceptual Scope

House defines "leadership" organizationally and narrowly as "the ability of an individual to influence, motivate, and enable others to contribute toward the effectiveness and success of the organizations of which they are members." Organizationally, leadership directly impacts the effectiveness of costs, revenue generation, service, satisfaction, earnings, market value, share price, social capital, motivation, engagement, and sustainability. Leadership is the ability of an individual to set rules for others and lead from the front. It is an attitude that influences the environment around us.

Compare the discussions on group leadership and ad hoc leadership above. One can also characterize leadership by the period of the authority, as in "During the 1940s Russia was under Stalinist leadership". In formal the term can also serve to describe the position or relationships which allow and legitimize the exercising of what one might term "leadership behavior". In some languages the term for a leader and the term for the principle of leadership have very different meanings. Furthermore, note the different connotations of a synonym of the word "leader" adopted from the German: the word Führer, and its accompanying ideas on the Führerprinzip.

In would-be controlling groups such as the military, political parties, ruling élites, and other belief-based enterprises like religions or businesses, the idea of leadership can become a Holy Grail and people can come to expect transformational change stemming from the leader; such entities may encourage their followers and believers to worship leadership, to respect it, and to strive (whether realistically or not) to become effective in it. Ideally, one cannot buy or sell leadership in the military; instead, leaders must ratify their position of command in the hearts and minds of their soldiers in order to obtain the best from them. Followers in such a situation may become uncritically obedient. Personal strategies that one can use to guard against the unrealistic expectations associated with belief in leaders include:

- maintaining a questioning attitude
- bolstering confidence in one's own decision-making abilities
- seeking independent verification through appropriate measurement and reporting infrastructures

Categories and Types of Leadership

Leadership is a quality a person may have. One can categorize the exercise of leadership as either actual or potential:

- actual-giving guidance or direction, as in the phrase "the emperor has provided satisfactory leadership".
- potential-the capacity or ability to lead, as in the phrase "she could have exercised effective leadership"; or in the concept "born to lead".

In both cases, as a result of the constancy of change some people detect within the late 20th and early 21st centuries, the act of learning appears fundamental to certain types of leading and leadership. When learning and leadership coalesce, one could characterize this as "learnership".

Leadership can have a formal aspect (as in most political or business leadership) or an informal one (as in most friendships). Speaking of "leadership" (the abstract term) rather than of "leading" (the action) usually implies that the entities doing the leading have some "leadership skills" or competencies.

The Psychology of Leadership

One of the differentiating factors between Management and Leadership is the ability or even necessity to Inspire. A Leader, one who can instill passion and direction to an individual or group of individuals, will be using Psychology to affect that group either consciously or unconsciously. Those who seem to be "Natural Leaders" and effectively inspire groups without really knowing the strategies or tactics used are considered Charismatic Leaders. The conscious Leader on the other hand applies a variety of psychological tactics that affect the "reactions" of a group to the environment they exist in.

In numerous "directive" (meaning to willfully direct as opposed to unconsciously do) Organizational psychology disciplines such as "Directive Communication" by Arthur F Carmazzi and theories like "The ripple effect" by Sigal Barsade, leadership is a product of awareness and command of the reactions and influences of a group on the individual as well as the individual on the group.

A Leader's successful application of directive organizational psychology by modifying specific leadership behaviors towards the group, will yield an Organizational culture that is in essence "inspired".

The Embodiment of Leadership

Most research into leadership mistakenly focused on cognitive and intellectual processes, forgetting the important fact that every cognitive process is an embodied process. In the book Leading People the Black Belt Way, Timothy Warneka accurately points out that, "Great leadership begins with the body."

People are living, organic beings, and medical research is increasingly recognizing the truth that mind and body are, in fact, one. While we often speak about mind and body as separate entities, great leaders understand that mind and body are, in reality, two sides of the same coin. Superior leaders recognize further that an awareness of their own physical selves is a critical component of their success. In a very real way, our toes, stomachs, and shoulders are on equal footing (pardon the pun) with our thoughts and ideas. As with any other tool, however, leaders must be trained to use embodied leadership technology appropriately and effectively.

In leadership, as in the martial arts, your stance is critical to your success. If you have a weak stance, then every way you lead will be fundamentally flawed. For example, if you have a weak stance in your emotional life, then you will have significant difficulties when you attempt to lead other people relationally. Recalling that we are embodied beings, I do not mean the word stance to be understood only metaphorically. I am also using the word stance in the literal sense, in terms of how leaders actually carry themselves physically when they lead others. Learning embodied stance will deepen your capacity for experiencing your own emotions, and better equip you to cope with the emotions of others, from the lighthearted to the highly conflicted. Your stance, you will learn, has a very literal, not to mention enormous impact on your ultimate success as a leader.

Leadership Associated with Positions of Authority

In On Heroes, Hero-Worship, and the Heroic in History, Thomas Carlyle demonstrated the concept of leadership associated with a position of authority. In praising Oliver Cromwell's use of power to bring King Charles I to trial and eventual beheading, he wrote the following: "Let us remark, meanwhile, how indispensable everywhere a King is, in all movements of men. It is strikingly shown, in this very War, what becomes of men when they cannot find a Chief Man, and their enemies can."

From this viewpoint, leadership emerges when an entity as "leader" contrives to receive deference from other entities who become "followers". And as the passage from Carlyle demonstrates, the process of getting deference can become competitive in that the emerging "leader" draws "followers" from the factions of the prior or alternative "leaders".

In representative democracies the people retain sovereignty (popular sovereignty) but delegate day-to-day administration and leadership to elected officials. In the United States, for example, the Constitution provides an example of recycling authority. In the Constitutional Convention of 1787, the American Founders rejected the idea of a monarch. But they still proposed leadership by people in positions of authority, with the authority split into three powers: in this case the legislative, the executive, and the judiciary. Under the American theory, the authority of the leadership derives from the power of the voters as conveyed through the electoral college. Many individuals share authority, including the many legislators in the Senate and the House of Representatives.

Leadership Cycles

If a group or an organization wants or expects identifiable leadership, it will require processes for appointing/acquiring and replacing leaders.

Traditional closed groups rely on bloodlines or seniority to select leaders and/or leadership candidates: monarchies, tribal chiefdoms, oligarchies and aristocratic societies rely on and often define their institutions by such methods.

Competence or perceived competence provides a possible basis for selecting leadership elites from a broader pool of potential talent. Political lobbying may prove necessary in electoral systems, but immediately demonstrated skill and character may secure leadership in smaller groups such as gangs.

Many organizations and groups aim to identify, grow, foster and promote what they see as leadership potential or ability-especially among younger members of society. See for example the Scouting movement. For a specific environment, see leadership development.

The issues of succession planning or of legitimation become important at times when leadership (particularly individual leadership) might or must change due to term-expiry, accident or senescence.

Titles Emphasizing Authority

At certain stages in their development, the hierarchies of social ranks implied different degrees or ranks of leadership in society. Thus a knight led fewer men in general than did a duke; a baronet might in theory control less land than an earl. See peerage for a systematization of this hierarchy, and order of precedence for links to various systems.

In the course of the 19th and 20th centuries, several political operators took non-traditional paths to become dominant in their societies. They or their systems often expressed a belief in strong individual leadership, but existing titles and labels ("King", "Emperor", "President" and so on) often seemed inappropriate, insufficient or downright inaccurate in some circumstances.

The formal or informal titles or descriptions they or their flunkies employed express and foster a general veneration for leadership of the inspired and autocratic variety. The definite article when used as part of the title (in languages which use definite articles) emphasizes the existence of a sole "true" leader.

Symbolism of Leadership

Various symbolic attributes-often varying according to the cultural milieu-mark out authority-figures and help make them seem special and revered or feared. For examples and discussion, see symbols of leadership.

Leadership among Primates

Richard Wrangham and Dale Peterson, in Demonic Males: Apes and the Origins of Human Violence present evidence that only humans and chimpanzees, among all the animals living on earth, share a similar tendency for a cluster of behaviors: violence, territoriality, and competition for uniting behind the one chief male of the land. This position is contentious. Many animals beyond apes are territorial, compete, exhibit violence, and have a social structure controlled by a dominant male (lions, wolves, etc.), suggesting Wrangham and Peterson's evidence is not empirical.

By comparison, bonobos, the second-closest species-relatives of man, do not unite behind the chief male of the land. The bonobos show deference to an alpha or top-ranking female that, with the support of her coalition of other females, can prove as strong as the strongest male in the land. Thus, if leadership amounts to getting the greatest number of followers, then among the bonobos, a female almost always exerts the strongest and most effective leadership. However, not all scientists agree on the allegedly "peaceful" nature of the bonobo or its reputation as a "hippie chimp".

Some have argued that, since the bonobo pattern inverts the dominant pattern among chimpanzees and men with regard to whether a female can get more followers than a male, humans and chimpanzees both likely inherited gender-bias against women from the ancestors of the chimpanzees; gender-bias features as a genetic condition of men. And the bias against women having leadership as a position of authority occurs in most cultures in the world. As of 2002, Sweden had the highest percentage of women in the legislature: but only 43%. And the United States, Andorra, Israel, Sierra Leone, and Ireland tied for 57th place with less than 15% of the legislature women. Admittedly, those percentages significantly outclass the occurrence of female chimpanzees becoming alpha of the community by getting the most followers, but similar trends exist in manifesting a general gender-bias across cultures against females gaining leadership as a position of authority over followers.

An alternative explanation suggests that those individuals best suited to lead the a group will somehow rise to the occasion and that followers (for some reason) will accept them as leaders or as proto-leaders. In this scenario, the traits of the leaders (such as gender, aggressiveness, etc.) will depend on the requirements of a given situation, and ongoing leadership may become extrapolated from a series of such situations.

In cultural anthropology, much speculation on the origins of human leadership relates to the perceived increasing need for dispute resolution in increasingly densely-populated and increasingly complex societies.

The image of swarms of lemmings which follow the first lemming off a cliff appears frequently in characterizing followers. The animal kingdom also provides the actual model of the bellwether function in a mob of sheep. And human society also offers many examples of emulation. The fashion industry, for example, depends on it. Fashion marketers design clothing for celebrities, then offer less expensive variations/imitations for those who emulate the celebrities.

Unintentional leadership can also occur from more pro-active forms followership. For example, in organizations which punish both leadership inaction and mistakes, and in which a predicament has no good solution, a common tendency involves declaring oneself a follower of someone else-metaphorically passing the buck.

Another example of followership without intentional leadership comes with the market leadership of a pioneering company, or the price leadership of a monopolist. Other companies will emulate a successful strategy, product, or price, but originators may certainly not desire this-in fact they often do all they can legally do to prevent such direct competition.

The term "leadership" sometimes applies (confusingly) to a winning position in a race. One can speak of a front-runner in a sprint or of the "leader" in an election or poll as in a position of leadership. But such "leadership" does not involve any influence processes, and the "leader" will have followers who may not willingly choose to function as followers. Once again: one can make an important distinction between "in the lead" and the process of leadership. Once again, leadership implies a relationship of power-the power to guide others. Leading from the front, in a military sense, may imply foolhardiness and unnecessary self-exposure to danger: these do not necessarily make for successful long-term leadership strategies.

Scope of Leadership

One can govern oneself, or one can govern the whole earth. In between, we may find leaders who operate primarily within:

- youth
- families
- bands
- tribes
- organizations
- states and nations
- empires

Intertwined with such categories, and overlapping them, we find (for example) religious leaders (potentially with their own internal hierarchies), work-place leaders (executives, officers, senior/upper managers, middle managers, staff-managers, line-managers, team-leaders, supervisors...) and leaders of voluntary associations.

Some anthropological ideas envisage a widespread (but by no means universal) pattern of progression in the organisation of society in ever-larger groups, with the needs and practices of leadership changing accordingly. Thus simple dispute resolution may become legalistic dispensation of justice before developing into proactive legislative activity. Some leadership careers parallel this sort of progression: today's school-board chairperson may become tomorrow's city councilor, then take in (say) a mayordom before graduating to nation-wide politics. Compare the cursus honorum in ancient Rome.

Orthogonality and Leadership

Those who sing the praises of leadership or of certain types of leadership may encounter problems in implementing consistent leadership structures. For example, a pyramidal structure in which authority consistently emanates from the summit can stifle initiative and leave no path for grooming future leaders in the ranks of subordinate levels. Similarly, a belief in universal direct democracy may become unwieldy, and a system consisting of nothing but representative leaders may well become stymied in committees.

Thus many leadership systems promote different rules for different levels of leadership. Hereditary autocrats meet in the United Nations on equal representative terms with elected governments in a collegial leadership. Or individual local democracies may assign some of their powers to temporary dictators in emergencies, as in ancient Rome. Hierarchies intermingle with equality of opportunity at different levels.

Support-structures for Leadership

Though advocates of the "big man" school of visionary leadership would have us believe that charisma and personality alone can work miracles, most leaders operate within a structure of supporters and executive agents who carry out and monitor the expressed or filtered-down will of the leader. This undercutting of the importance of leadership may serve as a reminder of the existence of the follower: compare followership. A more or less formal bureaucracy (in the Weberian sense) can throw up a colorless nonentity as an entirely effective leader: this phenomenon may occur (for example) in a politburo environment. Bureaucratic organizations can also raise incompetent people to levels of leadership (see Peter Principle).

In modern dynamic environments formal bureaucratic organizations have started to become less common because of their inability to deal with fast-changing circumstances. Most modern business organizations (and some government departments) encourage what they see as "leadership skills" and reward identified potential leaders with promotions.

In a potential down-side to this sort of development, a big-picture grand-vision leader may foster another sort of hierarchy: a fetish of leadership amongst subordinate sub-leaders, encouraged to seize resources for their own sub-empires and to apply to the supreme leader only for ultimate arbitration.

Some leaders build coalitions and alliances: political parties abound with this type of leader. Still others depend on rapport with the masses: they labor on the shop-floor or stand in the front-line of battle, leading by example.

Determining what makes "Effective Leadership"

In comparing various leadership styles in many cultures, academic studies have examined the patterns in which leadership emerges and then fades, other ways in which it maintains its effectiveness, sometimes by natural succession according to established rules, and sometimes by the imposition of brute force.

The simplest way to measure the effectiveness of leadership involves evaluating the size of the following that the leader can muster. By this standard, Adolf Hitler became a very effective leader for a period-even if through delusional promises and coercive techniques. However, this approach may measure power rather than leadership. To measure leadership more specifically, one may assess the extent of influence on the followers, that is, the amount of leading. Within an organizational context this means financially valuing productivity. Effective leaders generate higher productivity, lower costs, and more opportunities than ineffective leaders. Effective leaders create results, attain goal, realize vision, and other objectives more quickly and at a higher level of quality than ineffective leaders.

James MacGregor Burns introduced a normative element: an effective Burnsian leader will unite followers in a shared vision that will improve an organization and society at large. Burns calls leadership that delivers "true" value, integrity, and trust transformational leadership. He distinguishes such leadership from "mere" transactional leadership that builds power by doing whatever will get more followers. But problems arise in quantifying the transformational quality of leadership-evaluation of that quality seems more difficult to quantify than merely counting the followers that the straw man of transactional leadership James MacGregor Burns has set as a primary standard for effectiveness. Thus transformational leadership requires an evaluation of quality, independent of the market demand that exhibits in the number of followers.

Current assessments of transformational and transactional leadership commonly make use of the

Multifactor Leadership Questionnaire (MLQ), developed by Bass and Avolio in 1990 and revised in 1995. It measures five dimensions of transformational leadership:

1. idealized influence-attributions
2. idealized influence-behaviors
3. inspirational motivation
4. individualized consideration
5. intellectual stimulation

The three dimensions of transactional leadership measured by the MLQ cover:

1. contingent reward
2. management by exception (active)
3. management by exception (passive)

The functional leadership model conceives leadership as a set of behaviors that helps a group perform a task, reach their goal, or perform their function. In this model, effective leaders encourage functional behaviors and discourage dysfunctional ones.

In the path-goal model of leadership, developed jointly by Martin Evans and Robert House and based on the "Expectancy Theory of Motivation", a leader has the function of clearing the path toward the goal(s) of the group, by meeting the needs of subordinates.

Some commentators use the metaphor of an orchestral conductor to describe the quality of the leadership process. An effective leader resembles an orchestra conductor in some ways. He/she has to somehow get a group of potentially diverse and talented people-many of whom have strong personalities-to work together toward a common output. Will the conductor harness and blend all the gifts his or her players possess? Will the players accept the degree of creative expression they have? Will the audience enjoy the sound they make? The conductor may have a clear determining influence on all of these questions.

Suggested Qualities of Leadership

Studies of leadership have suggested qualities that people often associate with leadership. They include:

- Guiding others through modeling (in the sense of providing a role model) and through willingness to serve others first (compare followership)
- Technical/specific skill at some task at hand
- Initiative and entrepreneurial drive
- Charismatic inspiration-attractiveness to others and the ability to leverage this esteem to motivate others
- Preoccupation with a role-a dedication that consumes much of leaders' life-service to a cause
- A clear sense of purpose (or mission)-clear goals-focus-commitment
- Results-orientation-directing every action towards a mission-prioritizing activities to spend time where results most accrue
- Cooperation-work well with others
- Optimism-very few pessimists become leaders
- Rejection of determinism-belief in one's ability to "make a difference"
- Ability to encourage and nurture those that report to them-delegate in such a way as people will grow
- Role models-leaders may adopt a persona that encapsulates their mission and lead by example
- Self-knowledge (in non-bureaucratic structures)
- Self-awareness-the ability to "lead" (as it were) one's own self prior to leading other selves similarly

- With regards to people and to projects, the ability to choose winners-recognizing that, unlike with skills, one cannot (in general) teach attitude. Note that "picking winners" ("choosing winners") carries implications of gamblers' luck as well as of the capacity to take risks, but "true" leaders, like gamblers but unlike "false" leaders, base their decisions on realistic insight (and usually on many other factors partially derived from "real" wisdom).
- Understanding what others say, rather than listening to how they say things-this could partly sum this quality up as "walking in someone else's shoes" (to use a common cliché).

The approach of listing leadership qualities, often termed "trait theory", assumes certain traits or characteristics will tend to lead to effective leadership. Although trait theory has an intuitive appeal, difficulties may arise in proving its tenets, and opponents frequently challenge this approach. The "strongest" versions of trait theory see these "leadership characteristics" as innate, and accordingly labels some people as "born leaders" due to their psychological makeup. On this reading of the theory, leadership development involves identifying and measuring leadership qualities, screening potential leaders from non-leaders, then training those with potential.

David McClelland, a Harvard-based researcher in the psychology of power and achievement, saw leadership skills, not so much as a set of traits, but as a pattern of motives. He claimed that successful leaders will tend to have a high need for power, a low need for affiliation, and a high level of what he called activity inhibition (one might call it self-control).

Situational leadership theory offers an alternative approach. It proceeds from the assumption that different situations call for different characteristics. According to this group of theories, no single optimal psychographic profile of a leader exists. The situational leadership model of Hersey and Blanchard, for example, suggest four leadership-styles and four levels of follower-development. For effectiveness, the model posits that the leadership-style must match the appropriate level of followership-development. In this model, leadership behaviour becomes a function not only of the characteristics of the leader, but of the characteristics of followers as well. Other situational leadership models introduce a variety of situational variables. These determinants include:

- the nature of the task (structured or routine)
- organizational policies, climate, and culture
- the preferences of the leader's superiors
- the expectations of peers
- the reciprocal responses of followers

The contingency model of Vroom and Yetton uses other situational variables, including:

- the nature of the problem
- the requirements for accuracy
- the acceptance of an initiative
- time-constraints
- cost constraints

However one determines leadership behaviour, one can categorize it into various leadership styles. Many ways of doing this exist. For example, the Managerial Grid Model, a behavioral leadership-model developed by Robert Blake and Jane Mouton in 1964, suggests five different leadership styles, based on leaders' strength of concern for people and their concern for goal achievement.

Kurt Lewin, Ronald Lipitt, and R. K. White identified three leadership styles: authoritarian, democratic, and laissez-faire, based on the amount of influence and power exercised by the leader.

The Fiedler contingency model bases the leader's effectiveness on what Fred Fiedler called situational contingency. This results from the interaction of leadership style and situational favourableness (later called "situational control").

Leadership "Styles" (per House and Podsakoff)

In 1994 House and Podsakoff attempted to summarize the behaviors and approaches of "outstanding leaders" that they obtained from some more modern theories and research findings. These leadership behaviors and approaches do not constitute specific styles, but cumulatively they probably characterize the most effective style of today's leaders/ managers. The listed leadership "styles" cover:

1. *Vision.* Outstanding leaders articulate an ideological vision congruent with the deeply-held values of followers, a vision that describes a better future to which the followers have an alleged moral right.
2. *Passion and self-sacrifice.* Leaders display a passion for, and have a strong conviction of, what they regard as the moral correctness of their vision. They engage in outstanding or extraordinary behavior and make extraordinary self-sacrifices in the interest of their vision and mission.
3. *Confidence, determination, and persistence.* Outstanding leaders display a high degree of faith in themselves and in the attainment of the vision they articulate. Theoretically, such leaders need to have a very high degree of self-confidence and moral conviction because their mission usually challenges

the status quo and, therefore, may offend those who have a stake in preserving the established order.

4. *Image-building*. House and Podsakoff regard outstanding leaders as self-conscious about their own image. They recognize the desirability of followers perceiving them as competent, credible, and trustworthy.
5. *Role-modeling*. Leader-image-building sets the stage for effective role-modeling because followers identify with the values of role models whom they perceived in positive terms.
6. *External representation*. Outstanding leaders act as spokespersons for their respective organizations and symbolically represent those organizations to external constituencies.
7. *Expectations of and confidence in followers*. Outstanding leaders communicate expectations of high performance from their followers and strong confidence in their followers' ability to meet such expectations.
8. *Selective motive-arousal*. Outstanding leaders selectively arouse those motives of followers that the outstanding leaders see as of special relevance to the successful accomplishment of the vision and mission.
9. *Frame alignment*. To persuade followers to accept and implement change, outstanding leaders engage in "frame alignment". This refers to the linkage of individual and leader interpretive orientations such that some set of followers' interests, values, and beliefs, as well as the leader's activities, goals, and ideology, becomes congruent and complementary.
10. *Inspirational communication*. Outstanding leaders often, but not always, communicate their message in

an inspirational manner using vivid stories, slogans, symbols, and ceremonies.

Even though these ten leadership behaviors and approaches do not really equate to specific styles, evidence has started to accumulate that a leader's style can make a difference. Style becomes the key to the formulation and implementation of strategy and plays an important role in work-group members' activity and in team citizenship. Little doubt exists that the way (style) in which leaders influence work-group members can make a difference in their own and their people's performance. (Adopted from: Robert House and Philip M. Podsakoff, "Leadership Effectiveness: Past Perspectives and Future Directions for Research" in Jerald Greenberg (ed.), Organizational Behavior: The State of the Science, Erlbaum, Hillsdale, NJ., 1994, pp .)

Leadership and Vision

Many definitions of leadership involve an element of vision-except in cases of involuntary leadership and often in cases of traditional leadership. A vision provides direction to the influence process. A leader (or group of leaders) can have one or more visions of the future to aid them to move a group successfully towards this goal. A vision, for effectiveness, should allegedly:

- appear as a simple, yet vibrant, image in the mind of the leader
- describe a future state, credible and preferable to the present state
- act as a bridge between the current state and a future optimum state
- appear desirable enough to energize followers
- succeed in speaking to followers at an emotional or spiritual level (logical appeals by themselves seldom muster a following)

For leadership to occur, according to this theory, some people ("leaders") must communicate the vision to others ("followers") in such a way that the followers adopt the vision as their own. Leaders must not just see the vision themselves, they must have the ability to get others to see it also. Numerous techniques aid in this process, including: narratives, metaphors, symbolic actions, leading by example, incentives, and penalties.

Stacey (1992) has suggested that the emphasis on vision puts an unrealistic burden on the leader. Such emphasis appears to perpetuate the myth that an organization must depend on a single, uncommonly talented individual to decide what to do. Stacey claims that this fosters a culture of dependency and conformity in which followers take no pro-active incentives and do not think independently.

Kanungo's charismatic leadership model describes the role of the vision in three stages that are continuously ongoing, overlapping one another. Assessing the status quo, formulation and articulation of the vision, and implementation of the vision. This model suggests effective leadership needs these behaviors

Leadership's Relation with Management

Some commentators link leadership closely with the idea of management. Some regard the two as synonymous, and others consider management a subset of leadership. If one accepts this premise, one can view leadership as:

- centralized or decentralized
- broad or focused
- decision-oriented or morale-centred
- intrinsic or derived from some authority

Any of the bipolar labels traditionally ascribed to management style could also apply to leadership style.

Hersey and Blanchard use this approach: they claim that management merely consists of leadership applied to business situations; or in other words: management forms a sub-set of the broader process of leadership. They put it this way: "Leadership occurs any time one attempts to influence the behavior of an individual or group, regardless of the reason.... Management is a kind of leadership in which the achievement of organizational goals is paramount."

However, a clear distinction between management and leadership may nevertheless prove useful. This would allow for a reciprocal relationship between leadership and management, implying that an effective manager should possess leadership skills, and an effective leader should demonstrate management skills. One clear distinction could provide the following definition:

- Management involves power by position.
- Leadership involves power by influence.

Abraham Zaleznik (1977), for example, delineated differences between leadership and management. He saw leaders as inspiring visionaries, concerned about substance; while managers he views as planners who have concerns with process. Warren Bennis (1989) further explicated a dichotomy between managers and leaders. He drew twelve distinctions between the two groups:

- Managers administer, leaders innovate
- Managers ask how and when, leaders ask what and why
- Managers focus on systems, leaders focus on people
- Managers do things right, leaders do the right things
- Managers maintain, leaders develop
- Managers rely on control, leaders inspire trust
- Managers have a short-term perspective, leaders have a longer-term perspective

- Managers accept the status-quo, leaders challenge the status-quo
- Managers have an eye on the bottom line, leaders have an eye on the horizon
- Managers imitate, leaders originate
- Managers emulate the classic good soldier, leaders are their own person
- Managers copy, leaders show originality

Paul Birch (1999) also sees a distinction between leadership and management. He observed that, as a broad generalization, managers concerned themselves with tasks while leaders concerned themselves with people. Birch does not suggest that leaders do not focus on "the task." Indeed, the things that characterise a great leader include the fact that they achieve. Effective leaders create and sustain competitive advantage through the attainment of cost leadership, revenue leadership, time leadership, and market value leadership. Managers typically follow and realize a leader's vision. The difference lies in the leader realising that the achievement of the task comes about through the goodwill and support of others (influence), while the manager may not.

This goodwill and support originates in the leader seeing people as people, not as another resource for deployment in support of "the task". The manager often has the role of organizing resources to get something done. People form one of these resources, and many of the worst managers treat people as just another interchangeable item. A leader has the role of causing others to follow a path he/she has laid out or a vision he/she has articulated in order to achieve a task. Often, people see the task as subordinate to the vision. For instance, an organization might have the overall task of generating profit, but a good leader may see profit as a by-product that flows from whatever aspect of their vision differentiates their company from the competition.

Leadership does not only manifest itself as purely a business phenomenon. Many people can think of an inspiring leader they have encountered who has nothing whatever to do with business: a politician, an officer in the armed forces, a Scout or Guide leader, a teacher, etc. Similarly, management does not occur only as a purely business phenomenon. Again, we can think of examples of people that we have met who fill the management niche in non-business organisations. Non-business organizations should find it easier to articulate a non-money-driven inspiring vision that will support true leadership. However, often this does not occur.

Differences in the mix of leadership and management can define various management styles. Some management styles tend to de-emphasize leadership. Included in this group one could include participatory management, democratic management, and collaborative management styles. Other management styles, such as authoritarian management, micro-management, and top-down management, depend more on a leader to provide direction. Note, however, that just because an organisation has no single leader giving it direction, does not mean it necessarily has weak leadership.

In many cases group leadership (multiple leaders) can prove effective. Having a single leader (as in dictatorship) allows for quick and decisive decision-making when needed as well as when not needed. Group decision-making sometimes earns the derisive label "committee-itis" because of the longer times required to make decisions, but group leadership can bring more expertise, experience, and perspectives through a democratic process. Patricia Pitcher (1994) has challenged the bifurcation into leaders and managers. She used a factor analysis technique on data collected over 8 years, and concluded that three types of leaders exist, each with very different psychological profiles. She characterises one group as imaginative, inspiring, visionary, entrepreneurial, intuitive, daring, and emotional, and calls them "artists". In a second grouping she places "craftsmen" as well-balanced, steady, reasonable, sensible, predictable, and trustworthy. Finally she identifies "technocrats" as cerebral, detail-oriented, fastidious, uncompromising, and hard-headed. She speculates that no one profile offers a preferred leadership style. She claims that if we want to build, we should find an "artist leader"; if we want to solidify our position, we should find a "craftsman leader"; and if we have an ugly job that needs to get done (like downsizing), we should find a "technocratic leader." Pitcher also observed that a balanced leader exhibiting all three sets of traits occurs extremely rarely: she found none in her study.

Bruce Lynn postulates a differentiation between 'Leadership' and 'Management' based on perspectives to risk. Specifically, "A Leader optimises upside opportunity; a Manager minimises downside risk." He argues that successful executives need to apply both disciplines in a balance appropriate to the enterprise and its context. Leadership without Management yields steps forward, but as many if not more steps backwards. Management without Leadership avoids any step backwards, but doesn't move forward.

Leadership by a Group

In contrast to individual leadership, some organizations have adopted group leadership. In this situation, more than one person provides direction to the group as a whole. Some organizations have taken this approach in hopes of increasing creativity, reducing costs, or downsizing. Others may see the traditional leadership of a boss as costing too much in team performance. In some situations, the maintenance of the boss becomes too expensive-either by draining the resources of the group as a whole, or by impeding the creativity within the team, even unintentionally.

A common example of group leadership involves cross-functional teams. A team of people with diverse skills and from all parts of an organization assembles to lead a project. A team structure can involve sharing power equally on all issues, but more commonly uses rotating leadership. The team member(s) best able to handle any given phase of the project become(s) the temporary leader(s).

For example, the Orpheus orchestra has performed for over thirty years without a conductor--that is, without a sole leader. As a team of over 25 members, it has drawn discriminating audiences, and has produced over 60 recordings for Deutsche Grammophon in successful competition with other world-class orchestras.

Rather than an autocratic or charismatic conductor deciding the overall conception of a work and then dictating how each individual is to perform the individual tasks, the Orpheus team generally selects a different "core group" for each piece of music. The core group provides leadership in working out the details of the piece, and presents their ideas to the whole team. Members of the whole team then participate in refining the final conception, rehearsal, and product, including checking from various places in the auditorium how the sound balances and verifying the quality of the final recording.

At times the entire Orpheus team may follow a single leader, but whom the team follows rotates from task to task, depending on the capabilities of its members.

The orchestra has developed seminars and training sessions for adapting the Orpheus Process to business.

Co-leadership

As a compromise between individual leadership and an open group, leadership structures of two or three people or entities occur commonly. Ancient Rome preferred two consuls to a single king, and the Roman Empire grew to accommodate two Emperors-those of the East and of the West-simultaneously. The Middle Ages saw leadership divided between the secular and spiritual realms-between Emperor and Pope. Some groups-often left-wing or Green in orientation-employ a co-leader structure today.

Triumvirates have long served to balance leadership ambitions-notably in Rome in the first century BC, but also as recently as in the Soviet Union troikas of the 20th century. Compare the separation of powers (legislative, judicial and executive) formalised (for example) in the constitution of the United States of America.

Divided Leadership

Whereas sometimes one can readily and definitively identify the locus of leadership, in other circumstances the situation remains obscured. Pre-modern Japan offers a classical example: the emperors provided symbolic and religious leadership, but the shoguns embodied virtually all political and administrative leadership.

Similar dichotomies appear in many places and in many periods. Any constitutional monarch has a potentially confusing relationship with the day-to-day leader (typically a prime minister) who remains (at least theoretically) subordinate-socially as well as politically. Regents may stand against monarchs (and their supporters) during the minority or absence of those monarchs. Heads of state may operate at cross-purposes with heads of government (see governmental co-habitation). Political leaders may or may not align closely with religious leaders. And in federal-type systems, regional leadership and its potentially different systems may cross swords with national leaders. Not to mention the potentially conflicting leadership manifestations of boards of directors and of Chief Executives.

Historical views on Leadership

Aristocratic thinkers have postulated that leadership depends on one's blue blood or genes: monarchy takes an extreme view of the same idea, and may prop up its assertions against the claims of mere aristocrats by invoking divine sanction: see the divine right of kings. Contrariwise, more democratically-inclined theorists have pointed to examples of meritocratic leaders, such as the Napoleonic marshals profiting from careers open to talent.

In the autocratic/paternalistic strain of thought, traditionalists recall the role of leadership of the Roman pater familias. Feminist thinking, on the other hand, may damn such models as patriarchal and posit against them emotionally-attuned, responsive, and consensual empathetic guidance and matriarchies.

Comparable to the Roman tradition, the views of Confucianism on "right living" relate very much to the ideal of the (male) scholar-leader and his benevolent rule, buttressed by a tradition of filial piety.

Within the context of Islam, views on the nature, scope and inheritance of leadership have played a major role in shaping sects and their history. See caliphate.

In the 19th century, the elaboration of anarchist thought called the whole concept of leadership into question. (Note that the Oxford English Dictionary traces the word "leadership" in English only as far back as the 19th century.) One response to this denial of élitism came with Leninism, which demanded an élite group of disciplined cadres to act as the vanguard of a socialist revolution, bringing into existence the dictatorship of the proletariat. Other historical views of leadership have addressed the seeming contrasts between secular and religious leadership. The doctrines of Caesaro-papism have recurred and had their detractors over several centuries. Christian thinking on leadership has often emphasized stewardship of divinely-provided resources-human and material-and their deployment in accordance with a Divine plan. Compare servant leadership.

Alternatives to Leadership

Within groups, alternatives to the cult of leadership include using decision-making structures such as co-operative ventures, collegiality, consensus, anarchism and applied democracy. One can downplay the ubiquitous idea of leadership by using structures such as information clearing houses or stressing functions such as administration. Note the different implications and connotations of the two phrases "coalition of the willing" and "US-led coalition". The Orpheus Chamber Orchestra, which practices a form of distributed leadership, provides a textbook example of alternative leadership.

COORDINATION

Coordination is the act of coordinating, making different people or things work together for a goal or effect.

Coordination may also refer to:

- Coordination bond, a type of chemical bond
- Coordination game, a game in which all pure strategy Nash equilibria exist when players choose the same or corresponding strategies
- Coordination (linguistics), a compound grammatical construction
- Motor coordination, in animal motion

COLLABORATION

Collaboration is a structured, recursive process where two or more people work together toward a common goal-typically an intellectual endeavor that is creative in nature -by sharing knowledge, learning and building consensus. Collaboration does not require leadership and can even bring better results through decentralization and egalitarianism. In particular, teams that work collaboratively can obtain greater resources, recognition and reward when facing competition for finite resources.

Structured methods of collaboration encourage introspection of behavior and communication. These methods specifically aim to increase the success of teams as they engage in collaborative problem solving. Forms, rubrics, charts and graphs are useful in these situations to objectively document personal traits with the goal of improving performance in current and future projects.

Since the Second World War the term "Collaboration" acquired a very negative meaning as referring to persons and groups which help a foreign occupier of their country-due to actual use by people in France and other European countries who worked with and for the Nazi German occupiers. Lingusitically, "collaboration" implies more ar less equal partners who work together-which is obviously not the case when one party is an army of occupation and the other are people of the occupied country living under the power of this army. In order to make a distinction, the more specific term "Collaborationism" is often used for this phenomenon of collaboration with an occupying army. However, there is no water-tight distinction; "Collaboration" and "Collaborator", as well as "Collaborationism" and "Collaborationist", are often used in this pejorative sense-and even more so, the equivalent terms in French and other languages spoken in countries which experienced direct Nazi occupation.

History

Trade

Trade originated with the start of communication in prehistoric times. Trading was the main facility of prehistoric people, who bartered goods and services from each other when there was no such thing as the modern day currency. Peter Watson dates the history of long-distance commerce from circa 150,000 years ago.

Trade exists for many reasons. Due to specialisation and division of labor, most people concentrate on a small aspect of production, trading for other products. Trade exists between regions because different regions have a comparative advantage in the production of some tradable commodity, or because different regions' size allows for the benefits of mass production. As such, trade at market prices between locations benefits both locations.

Community Organization

An intentional community is a planned residential community designed to promote a much higher degree of social interaction than other communities. The members of an intentional community typically hold a common social, political or spiritual vision. They also share responsibilities and resources. Intentional communities include cohousing, residential land trusts, ecovillages, communes, kibbutzim, ashrams, and housing cooperatives. Typically, new members of an intentional community are selected by the community's existing membership, rather than by real-estate agents or land owners (if the land is not owned by the community).

Hutterite, Austria (1500s)

Hutterites practice a near-total community of goods: all property is owned by the colony, and provisions for individual members and their families come from the common resources. This practice is based largely on Hutterite interpretation of passages in chapters 2, 4, and 5 of Acts, which speak of the believers "having all things in common". Thus the colony owns and operates its buildings and equipment like a corporation. Housing units are built and assigned to individual families but belong to the colony and there is very little personal property. Meals are taken by the entire colony in a common long room.

Oneida Community, Oneida, New York (1848)

The Oneida Community practiced Communalism (in the sense of communal property and possessions) and Mutual Criticism, where every member of the community was subject to criticism by committee or the community as a whole, during a general meeting. The goal was to eliminate bad character traits.

Early Kibbutz Settlements Founded near Jerusalem (1890)

A Kibbutz is an Israeli collective community. The movement combines socialism and Zionism in a form of practical Labor Zionism, founded at a time when independent farming was not practical or perhaps more correctly-not practicable. Forced by necessity into communal life, and inspired by their own ideology, the kibbutz members developed a pure communal mode of living that attracted interest from the entire world. While the kibbutzim lasted for several generations as utopian communities, most of today's kibbutzim are scarcely different from the capitalist enterprises and regular towns to which the kibbutzim were originally supposed to be alternatives.

Modern Art

- DADA-Switzerland
- Impressionists Paris
- Islington, London
- Modernists Russia

Game Theory

Game theory is a branch of applied mathematics and economics that looks at situations where multiple players make decisions in an attempt to maximize their returns. The first documented discussion of it is a letter written by James Waldegrave in 1713. Antoine Augustin Cournot's Researches into the Mathematical Principles of the Theory of Wealth in 1838 provided the first general theory. It was not until 1928 that this became a recognized, unique field when John von Neumann published a series of papers. Von Neumann's work in game theory culminated in the 1944 book The Theory of Games and Economic Behavior by von Neumann and Oskar Morgenstern. In 1950, the first discussion of the prisoner's dilemma appeared, and an experiment was undertaken on this game at the RAND corporation.

Military-industrial Complex

The term military-industrial complex refers to a close and symbiotic relationship among a nation's armed forces, its private industry, and associated political and commercial interests. In such a system, the military is dependent on industry to supply material and other support, while the defense industry depends on government for revenue.

Skunk Works

Skunk Works is a term used in engineering and technical fields to describe a group within an organization given a high degree of autonomy and unhampered by bureaucracy, tasked with working on advanced or secret projects. Founded at Lockheed Martin in 1943, the team developed highly innovative aircraft in short time frames, even beating its first deadline by 37 days. Creator of the organization, Kelly Johnson is said to have been an 'organizing genius' and had fourteen basic operating rules.

Manhattan Project

The Manhattan Project was the project to develop the first nuclear weapon (atomic bomb) during World War II by the United States, the United Kingdom and Canada. Formally designated as the Manhattan Engineer District (MED), it refers specifically to the period of the project from 1941-1946 under the control of the U.S. Army Corps of Engineers, under the administration of General Leslie R. Groves. The scientific research was directed by American physicist J. Robert Oppenheimer.

While the aforementioned persons were influential in the project itself, the value of this project as an influence on organized collaboration is better attributed to Vannevar Bush. In early 1940, bush lobbied for the creation of the National Defense Research Committee. Frustrated by previous bureaucratic failures in implementing technology in World War I, Bush sought to organize the scientific power of the United States for greater success.

The project succeeded in developing and detonating three nuclear weapons in 1945: a test detonation of a plutonium implosion bomb on July 16 (the Trinity test) near Alamogordo, New Mexico; an enriched uranium bomb code-named "Little Boy" on August 6 over Hiroshima, Japan; and a second plutonium bomb, code-named "Fat Man" on August 9 over Nagasaki, Japan.

Project Management

As a discipline, Project Management developed from different fields of application including construction, engineering, and defense. In the United States, the forefather of project management is Henry Gantt, called the father of planning and control techniques, who is famously known for his use of the "bar" chart as a project management tool, for being an associate of Frederick Winslow Taylor's theories of scientific management, and for his study of the work and management of Navy ship building. His work is the forerunner to many modern project management tools including the work breakdown structure (WBS) and resource allocation.

The 1950s marked the beginning of the modern project management era. Again, in the United States, prior to the 1950s, projects were managed on an ad hoc basis using mostly Gantt charts, and informal techniques and tools. At that time, two mathematical project scheduling models were developed:

(1) the "Program Evaluation and Review Technique" or PERT, developed as part of the United States Navy's (in conjunction with the Lockheed Corporation) Polaris missile submarine program; and

(2) the "Critical Path Method" (CPM) developed in a joint venture by both DuPont Corporation and Remington Rand Corporation for managing plant maintenance projects. These mathematical techniques quickly spread into many private enterprises.

In 1969, the Project Management Institute (PMI) was formed to serve the interest of the project management industry. The premise of PMI is that the tools and techniques of project management are common even among the widespread application of projects from the software industry to the construction industry. In 1981, the PMI Board of Directors authorized the development of what has become A Guide to the Project Management Body of Knowledge (PMBOK), containing the standards and guidelines of practice that are widely used throughout the profession. The International Project Management Association (IPMA), founded in Europe in 1967, has undergone a similar development and instituted the IPMA Project Baseline.

Both organizations are now participating in the development of a global project management standard.

Art Groups

Fluxus

An international network of artists, composers and designers noted for blending different artistic media and disciplines in the 1960s. Fluxus encouraged a do it yourself aesthetic, and valued simplicity over complexity. Like Dada before it, Fluxus included a strong current of anti-commercialism and an anti-art sensibility, disparaging the conventional market-driven art world in favor of an artist-centered creative practice. As Fluxus artist Robert Filliou wrote, however, Fluxus differed from Dada in its richer set of aspirations, and the positive social and communitarian aspirations of Fluxus far outweighed the anti-art tendency that also marked the group.

Situationist International

The Situationist International (SI) was a small group of international political and artistic agitators with roots in Marxism, Lettrism and the early 20th century European artistic and political avant-gardes. Formed in 1957, the SI was active in Europe through the 1960s and aspired to major social and political transformations. In the 1960s it split into a number of different groups, including the Situationist Bauhaus, the Antinational and the Second Situationist International. The first SI disbanded in 1972.

Feminism

The Woman's Building was a non-profit public art and educational center focused on showcasing women's art and culture. It existed in Los Angeles from 1973 to 1991. Womanhouse, an installation organized by this center in 1972, encouraged participants to work together.

Back-to-the-land Movement

- 1960s, 1970s-beginning in the USA, this is a movement generally known to be from 'hippies.'

Academia

Black Mountain College

Founded in 1933 by John Andrew Rice, Theodore Dreier and other former faculty of Rollins College, Black Mountain was experimental by nature and committed to an interdisciplinary approach, attracting a faculty which included many of America's leading visual artists, poets, and designers.

Operating in a relatively isolated rural location with little budget, Black Mountain College inculcated an informal and collaborative spirit, and over its lifetime attracted a venerable roster of instructors. Some of the innovations, relationships and unexpected connections formed at Black Mountain would prove to have a lasting influence on the postwar American art scene, high culture, and eventually pop culture. Buckminster Fuller met student Kenneth Snelson at Black Mountain, and the result was the first geodesic dome (improvised out of slats in the school's back yard); Merce Cunningham formed his dance company; and John Cage staged his first happening.

Not a haphazardly conceived venture, Black Mountain College was a consciously directed liberal arts school that grew out of the progressive education movement. In its day it was a unique educational experiment for the artists and writers who conducted it, and as such an important incubator for the American avant garde. Black Mountain proved to be an important precursor to and prototype for many of the alternative colleges of today ranging from the University of California, Santa Cruz to Hampshire College and Evergreen State College, among others.

Learning Community

Dr. Wolff-Michael Roth and Stuart Lee of the University of Victoria assert that until the early 1990s the individual was the 'unit of instruction' and the focus of research. The two observed that researchers and practitioners switched to the idea that knowing is 'better' thought of as a cultural practice. Roth and Lee also claim that this led to changes in learning and teaching design in which students were encouraged to share their ways of doing mathematics, history, science, with each other. In other words, that children take part in the construction of consensual domains, and 'participate in the negotiation and institutionalisation of ... meaning'. In effect, they are participating in learning communities.

This analysis does not take account of the appearance of Learning communities in the United States in the early 1980s. For example, The Evergreen State College, which is widely considered a pioneer in this area, established an intercollegiate learning community in 1984. In 1985, this same college established the Washington Center for Improving the Quality of Undergraduate Education, which focuses on collaborative education approaches, including learning communities as one of its centerpieces.

Contemporary Examples

Arts

Collaboration-or joint production by two or more artists-is a common style among musicians and performance artists. It has not been so popular, on the other hand, in the world of art, and especially in modern art. But the strong sense of individualism long possessed by artists of fine art began to wane around the 1960s, and some artists working in units have emerged and become widely known along with the development of new media based on the advances in information technology. They have changed the concept of art into something that can be engaged in by more than individual artists alone.

Business

Collaboration in business can be found both inter-and intra-organization and ranges from the simplicity of a partnership to the complexity of a multinational corporation.

COOPERATION

This article is about cooperation as used in the social sciences. For co-operation in evolution, see Co-operation (evolution). For the economic model, see Cooperative.

Cooperation, co-operation or coöperation is the practice of individuals or larger societal entities working in common with mutually agreed-upon goals and possibly methods, instead of working separately in competition, and in which the success of one is dependent and contingent upon the success of another.

Cooperation, more formally speaking is how the components of a system work together to achieve the global properties. In other words, individual components that appear to be "selfish" and independent work together to create a highly complex, greater-than-the-sum-of-its-parts system. Examples can be found all around us. The components in a cell work together to keep it living. Cells work together and communicate to produce multicellular organisms. Organisms form food chains and ecosystems. People form families, gangs, cities and nations. Neurons create thought and consciousness. Understanding the mechanisms that create cooperating agents in a system is one of the most important and least well understood phenomena in nature, though there has not been a lack of effort.

However, co-operation may be coerced (forced) or voluntary (freely chosen), and consequently individuals and groups might co-operate even although they have almost nothing in common qua interests or goals. Examples of that can be found in market trade, military wars, families, workplaces, schools and prisons, and more generally any institution or organisation of which individuals are part (out of own choice, by law, or forced).

Cooperation vs. Competition

While cooperation is the antithesis of competition, the need or desire to compete with others is a common impetus that motivates individuals to organize into a group and cooperate with each other in order to form a stronger competitive force.

Coöperation in many areas such as farming and housing may be in the form of a cooperative or, alternately, in the form of a conventional business.

Many people resort to this because, they may cooperate by trading with each other or by altruistic sharing.

Certain forms of cooperation are illegal in some jurisdictions because they alter the nature of access by others to economic or other resources. Thus, cooperation in the form of cartels or price-fixing may be illegal.

A few mechanisms have been suggested for the appearance of cooperation between humans or in natural system

The Prisoner's Dilemma

Even if all members of a group would benefit if all cooperate, individual self-interest may not favor cooperation. The prisoner's dilemma codifies this problem and has been the subject of much research, both theoretical and experimental. Results from experimental economics show that humans often act more cooperatively than strict self-interest would seem to dictate.

One reason for this may be that if the prisoner's dilemma situation is repeated (the iterated prisoner's dilemma), it allows non-cooperation to be punished more, and cooperation to be rewarded more, than the single-shot version of the problem would suggest. It has been suggested that this is one reason for the evolution of complex emotional and social behavior in higher animals.

Another reason might be that humans are by nature socially co-operative beings, who, at least as infants, and usually thereafter, cannot survive without co-operating-although with maturation they gain much more choice about the kinds of co-operation they wish to have.

There are four main conditions that tend to be necessary for cooperative behaviour to develop between two individuals:

- An overlap in desires
- A chance of future encounters with the same individual
- Memory of past encounters with that individual
- A value associated with future outcomes

6

CONTROL MANAGEMENT

Control in one of the managerial functions like planning, organising, staffing and directing. It is an important function because it helps to check the errors and to take the corrective action so that deviation from standards are minimised and stated goals of the organisation are achieved in desired manner.

According to modern concepts, control is a foreseeing action whereas earlier concept of control was used only when errors were detected. Control in management means setting standards, measuring actual performance and taking corrective action. Thus, control comprises these three main activities.

Definitions

According to Henry Fayol,

Control of an undertaking consists of seeing that everything is being carried out in accordance with the plan which has been adopted, the orders which have been given, and the principles which have been laid down. Its object is to point out mistakes in order that they may be rectified and prevented from recurring.

According to EFL Breach,

Control is checking current performance against predetermined standards contained in the plans, with aview to ensure adequate progress and satisfactory performance.

According to Harold Koontz,

Controlling is the measurement and correction of performance in order to make sure that enterprise objectives and the plans devised to attain them are accomplished.

According to Stafford Beer,

Management is the profession of control.

From these definitions it can be stated that there is close link between planning and controlling. Planning is a process by which an organisation's objectives and the methods to achieve the objectives are established, and controlling is a process which measures and directs the actual performance against the planned objectives of the organisation. Thus, planning and control are often referred to as siamese twins of management.

Characteristics of Control

- Control is a continuous process
- Control is a management process
- Control is embedded in each level of organisational hierarchy
- Control is forward looking
- Control is closely linked with planning
- Controling is tool for achieving organisational activities

CONTROL PREMIUM

Control premium is an amount that a buyer is usually willing to pay over the current market price of a company. This premium is justified by the expected synergies, such as the expected increase in cash flow resulting from cost savings and revenue enhancements achievable in the merger. Normally, the control premium is industry-specific and amounts to 20-30% of the market price.

Mergers and Acquisitions

The phrase mergers and acquisitions (abbreviated M&A) refers to the aspect of corporate strategy, corporate finance and management dealing with the buying, selling and combining of different companies that can aid, finance, or help a growing company in a given industry grow rapidly without having to create another business entity.

Overview

Merger is a tool used by companies for the purpose of expanding their operations often aiming at an increase of their long term profitability. There are 15 different types of actions that a company can take when deciding to move forward using M&A. Usually mergers occur in a consensual (occurring by mutual consent) setting where executives from the target company help those from the purchaser in a due diligence process to ensure that the deal is beneficial to both parties. Acquisitions can also happen through a hostile takeover by purchasing the majority of outstanding shares of a company in the open market against the wishes of the target's board. In the United States, business laws vary from state to state whereby some companies have limited protection against hostile takeovers. One form of protection against a hostile takeover is the shareholder rights plan, otherwise known as the "poison pill".

Historically, mergers have often failed (Straub, 2007) to add significantly to the value of the acquiring firm's shares (King, et al., 2004). Corporate mergers may be aimed at reducing market competition, cutting costs (for example, laying off employees, operating at a more technologically efficient scale, etc.), reducing taxes, removing management, "empire building" by the acquiring managers, or other purposes which may or may not be consistent with public policy or public welfare. Thus they can be heavily regulated, for example, in the U.S. requiring approval by both the Federal Trade Commission and the Department of Justice.

The U.S. began their regulation on mergers in 1890 with the implementation of the Sherman Act. It was meant to prevent any attempt to monopolize or to conspire to restrict trade. However, based on the loose interpretation of the standard "Rule of Reason", it was up to the judges in the U.S. Supreme Court whether to rule leniently (as with U.S. Steel in 1920) or strictly (as with Alcoa in 1945).

Acquisition

An acquisition, also known as a takeover, is the buying of one company (the 'target') by another. An acquisition may be friendly or hostile. In the former case, the companies cooperate in negotiations; in the latter case, the takeover target is unwilling to be bought or the target's board has no prior knowledge of the offer. Acquisition usually refers to a purchase of a smaller firm by a larger one. Sometimes, however, a smaller firm will acquire management control of a larger or longer established company and keep its name for the combined entity. This is known as a reverse takeover.

Types of Acquisition

- The buyer buys the shares, and therefore control, of the target company being purchased. Ownership control of the company in turn conveys effective control over the assets of the company, but since the company is acquired intact as a going business, this form of transaction carries with it all of the liabilities accrued by that business over its past and all of the risks that company faces in its commercial environment.

- The buyer buys the assets of the target company. The cash the target receives from the sell-off is paid back to its shareholders by dividend or through liquidation. This type of transaction leaves the target company as an empty shell, if the buyer buys out the entire assets. A buyer often structures the transaction as an asset purchase to "cherry-pick" the assets that it wants and leave out the assets and liabilities that it does not. This can be particularly important where foreseeable liabilities may include future, unquantified damage awards such as those that could arise from litigation over defective products, employee benefits or terminations, or environmental damage. A disadvantage of this structure is the tax that many jurisdictions, particularly outside the United States, impose on transfers of the individual assets, whereas stock transactions can frequently be structured as like-kind exchanges or other arrangements that are tax-free or tax-neutral, both to the buyer and to the seller's shareholders.

The terms "demerger", "spin-off" and "spin-out" are sometimes used to indicate a situation where one company splits into two, generating a second company separately listed on a stock exchange.

Merger

In business or economics a merger is a combination of two companies into one larger company. Such actions are commonly voluntary and involve stock swap or cash payment to the target. Stock swap is often used as it allows the shareholders of the two companies to share the risk involved in the deal. A merger can resemble a takeover but result in a new company name (often combining the names of the original companies) and in new branding; in some cases, terming the combination a "merger" rather than an acquisition is done purely for political or marketing reasons.

Classifications of Mergers

- Horizontal mergers take place where the two merging companies produce similar product in the same industry.
- Vertical mergers occur when two firms, each working at different stages in the production of the same good, combine.
- Congeneric mergers occur where two merging firms are in the same general industry, but they have no mutual buyer/customer or supplier relationship, such as a merger between a bank and a leasing company. Example: Prudential's acquisition of Bache & Company.
- Conglomerate mergers take place when the two firms operate in different industries.

A unique type of merger called a reverse merger is used as a way of going public without the expense and time required by an IPO. The contract vehicle for achieving a merger is a "merger sub".

The occurrence of a merger often raises concerns in antitrust circles. Devices such as the Herfindahl index can analyze the impact of a merger on a market and what, if any, action could prevent it. Regulatory bodies such as the European Commission, the United States Department of Justice and the U.S. Federal Trade Commission may investigate anti-trust cases for monopolies dangers, and have the power to block mergers.

Accretive mergers are those in which an acquiring company's earnings per share (EPS) increase. An alternative way of calculating this is if a company with a high price to earnings ratio (P/E) acquires one with a low P/E. Dilutive mergers are the opposite of above, whereby a company's EPS decreases. The company will be one with a low P/E acquiring one with a high P/E.

The completion of a merger does not ensure the success of the resulting organization; indeed, many mergers (in some industries, the majority) result in a net loss of value due to problems. Correcting problems caused by incompatibility-whether of technology, equipment, or corporate culture-diverts resources away from new investment, and these problems may be exacerbated by inadequate research or by concealment of losses or liabilities by one of the partners. Overlapping subsidiaries or redundant staff may be allowed to continue, creating inefficiency, and conversely the new management may cut too many operations or personnel, losing expertise and disrupting employee culture. These problems are similar to those encountered in takeovers. For the merger not to be considered a failure, it must increase shareholder value faster than if the companies were separate, or prevent the deterioration of shareholder value more than if the companies were separate.

Business Valuation

The five most common ways to valuate a business are asset valuation, historical earnings valuation, future maintainable earnings valuation, Earnings Before Interest Taxes Depreciation and Amortization (EBITDA) valuation and Shareholder's Discretionary Cash Flow (SDCF) valuation. Professionals who valuate businesses generally do not use just one of these methods but a combination of some of them, as well as possibly others that are not mentioned above, in order to obtain a more accurate value. These values are determined for the most part by looking at a company's balance sheet and/or income statement and withdrawing the appropriate information. The information in the balance sheet or income statement is obtained by one of three accounting measures: a Notice to Reader, a Review Engagement or an Audit.

Accurate business valuation is one of the most important aspects of M&A as valuations like these will have a major impact on the price that a business will be sold for. Most often this information is expressed in a Letter of Opinion of Value (LOV) when the business is being valuated for interest's sake. There are other, more detailed ways of expressing the value of a business. These reports generally get more detailed and expensive as the size of a company increases, however, this is not always the case as there are many complicated industries which require more attention to detail, regardless of size.

Financing M&A

Mergers are generally differentiated from acquisitions partly by the way in which they are financed and partly by the relative size of the companies. Various methods of financing an M&A deal exist:

Cash

Payment by cash. Such transactions are usually termed acquisitions rather than mergers because the shareholders of the target company are removed from the picture and the target comes under the (indirect) control of the bidder's shareholders alone.

A cash deal would make more sense during a downward trend in the interest rates. Another advantage of using cash for an acquisition is that there tends to lesser chances of EPS dilution for the acquiring company. But a caveat in using cash is that it places constraints on the cash flow of the company.

Financing

Financing capital may be borrowed from a bank, or raised by an issue of bonds. Alternatively, the acquirer's stock may be offered as consideration. Acquisitions financed through debt are known as leveraged buyouts (only if they take the target private), and the debt will often be moved down onto the balance sheet of the acquired company.

Hybrids

An acquisition can involve a combination of cash and debt, or a combination of cash and stock of the purchasing entity.

Motives behind M&A

These motives are considered to add shareholder value:

- *Economies of scale*: This refers to the fact that the combined company can often reduce duplicate departments or operations, lowering the costs of the company relative to the same revenue stream, thus increasing profit.
- *Increased revenue/Increased Market Share*: This motive assumes that the company will be absorbing a major competitor and thus increase its power (by capturing increased market share) to set prices.
- *Cross selling*: For example, a bank buying a stock broker could then sell its banking products to the stock broker's customers, while the broker can sign up the bank's customers for brokerage accounts. Or, a manufacturer can acquire and sell complementary products.
- *Synergy*: Better use of complementary resources.
- *Taxes*: A profitable company can buy a loss maker to use the target's loss as their advantage by reducing their tax liability. In the United States and many other countries, rules are in place to limit the ability of profitable companies to "shop" for loss making companies, limiting the tax motive of an acquiring company.

- *Geographical or other diversification*: This is designed to smooth the earnings results of a company, which over the long term smoothens the stock price of a company, giving conservative investors more confidence in investing in the company. However, this does not always deliver value to shareholders (see below).
- *Resource transfer*: resources are unevenly distributed across firms (Barney, 1991) and the interaction of target and acquiring firm resources can create value through either overcoming information asymmetry or by combining scarce resources.
- *Increased Market share, which can increase market power*: In an oligopoly market, increased market share generally allows companies to raise prices. Note that while this may be in the shareholders' interest, it often raises antitrust concerns, and may not be in the public interest.

These motives are considered to not add shareholder value:

- *Diversification*: While this may hedge a company against a downturn in an individual industry it fails to deliver value, since it is possible for individual shareholders to achieve the same hedge by diversifying their portfolios at a much lower cost than those associated with a merger.
- *Manager's hubris*: manager's overconfidence about expected synergies from M&A which results in overpayment for the target company.
- *Empire building*: Managers have larger companies to manage and hence more power.
- *Manager's compensation*: In the past, certain executive management teams had their payout based

on the total amount of profit of the company, instead of the profit per share, which would give the team a perverse incentive to buy companies to increase the total profit while decreasing the profit per share (which hurts the owners of the company, the shareholders); although some empirical studies show that compensation is linked to profitability rather than mere profits of the company.

- *Vertical integration*: Companies acquire part of a supply chain and benefit from the resources. However this in turn does not add any value because as one end of the supply chain may receive product at a cheaper cost the other end now has lower revenue. In addition, the supplier may find more difficulty in supplying to competitors of its acquirer because the competition would not want to support the new conglomerate.

M&A Marketplace Difficulties

No marketplace currently exists for the mergers and acquisitions of privately owned small to mid-sized companies. Market participants often wish to maintain a level of secrecy about their efforts to buy or sell such companies. Their concern for secrecy usually arises from the possible negative reactions a company's employees, bankers, suppliers, customers and others might have if the effort or interest to seek a transaction were to become known. This need for secrecy has thus far thwarted the emergence of a public forum or marketplace to serve as a clearinghouse for this large volume of business.

At present, the process by which a company is bought or sold can prove difficult, slow and expensive. A transaction typically requires six to nine months and involves many steps. Locating parties with whom to conduct a transaction forms one step in the overall process and perhaps the most difficult one. Qualified and interested buyers of multimillion dollar corporations are hard to find. Even more difficulties attend bringing a number of potential buyers forward simultaneously during negotiations. Potential acquirers in industry simply cannot effectively "monitor" the economy at large for acquisition opportunities even though some may fit well within their company's operations or plans.

An industry of professional "middlemen" (known variously as intermediaries, business brokers, and investment bankers) exists to facilitate M&A transactions. These professionals do not provide their services cheaply and generally resort to previously-established personal contacts, direct-calling campaigns, and placing advertisements in various media. In servicing their clients they attempt to create a one-time market for a one-time transaction. Many, but not all, transactions use intermediaries on one or both sides. Despite best intentions, intermediaries can operate inefficiently because of the slow and limiting nature of having to rely heavily on telephone communications. Many phone calls fail to contact with the intended party. Busy executives tend to be impatient when dealing with sales calls concerning opportunities in which they have no interest. These marketing problems typify any private negotiated markets. Due to these problems and other problems like these, brokers who deal with small to mid-sized companies often deal with much more strenuous conditions than other business brokers. Mid-sized business brokers have an average life-span of only 12-18 months and usually never grow beyond 1 or 2 employees. Exceptions to this are few and far between. Some of these exceptions include The Sundial Group, Geneva Business Services and Robbinex.

The market inefficiencies can prove detrimental for this important sector of the economy. Beyond the intermediaries' high fees, the current process for mergers and acquisitions has the effect of causing private companies to initially sell their shares at a significant discount relative to what the same company might sell for were it already publicly traded. An important and large sector of the entire economy is held back by the difficulty in conducting corporate M&A (and also in raising equity or debt capital). Furthermore, it is likely that since privately held companies are so difficult to sell they are not sold as often as they might or should be.

Previous attempts to streamline the M&A process through computers have failed to succeed on a large scale because they have provided mere "bulletin boards"-static information that advertises one firm's opportunities. Users must still seek other sources for opportunities just as if the bulletin board were not electronic. A multiple listings service concept was previously not used due to the need for confidentiality but there are currently several in operation. The most significant of these are run by the California Association of Business Brokers (CABB) and the International Business Brokers Association (IBBA) These organizations have effectivily created a type of vitural market without compromising the confidentiality of parties involved and without the unauthorized release of information.

One part of the M&A process which can be improved significantly using networked computers is the improved access to "data rooms" during the due diligence process however only for larger transactions. For the purposes of small-medium sized business, these datarooms serve no purpose and are generally not used. Reasons for frequent failure of M&A was analyzed by Thomas Straub in "Reasons for frequent failure in mergers and acquisitions-a comprehensive analysis", DUV Gabler Edition, 2007.

The Great Merger Movement

The Great Merger Movement was a predominantly U.S. business phenomenon that happened from 1895 to 1905.

During this time, small firms with little market share consolidated with similar firms to form large, powerful institutions that dominated their markets. The vehicle used were so-called trusts. To truly understand how large this movement was-in 1900 the value of firms acquired in mergers was 20% of GDP. In 1990 the value was only 3% and from 1998-2000 is was around 10-11% of GDP. Organizations that commanded the greatest share of the market in 1905 saw that command disintegrate by 1929 as smaller competitors joined forces with each other.

Short-run Factors

One of the major short run factors that sparked in The Great Merger Movement was the desire to keep prices high. That is, with many firms in a market, supply of the product remains high. During the panic of 1893, the demand declined. When demand for the good falls, as illustrated by the classic supply and demand model, prices are driven down. To avoid this decline in prices, firms found it profitable to collude and manipulate supply to counter any changes in demand for the good. This type of cooperation led to widespread horizontal integration amongst firms of the era. Focusing on mass production allowed firms to reduce unit costs to a much lower rate. These firms usually were capital-intensive and had high fixed costs. Due to the fact of new machines were mostly financed through bonds, interest payments on bonds were high followed by the panic of 1893, yet no firm was willing to accept quantity reduction during this period.

Long-run Factors

In the long run, due to the desire to keep costs low, it was advantageous for firms to merge and reduce their transportation costs thus producing and transporting from one location rather than various sites of different companies as in the past. This resulted in shipment directly to market from this one location. In addition, technological changes prior to the merger movement within companies increased the efficient size of plants with capital intensive assembly lines allowing for economies of scale. Thus improved technology and transportation were forerunners to the Great Merger Movement. In part due to competitors as mentioned above, and in part due to the government, however, many of these initially successful mergers were eventually dismantled. The U.S. government passed the Sherman Act in 1890, setting rules against price fixing and monopolies. Starting in the 1890s with such cases as U.S. versus Addyston Pipe and Steel Co., the courts attacked large companies for strategizing with others or within their own companies to maximize profits. Price fixing with competitors created a greater incentive for companies to unite and merge under one name so that they were not competitors anymore and technically not price fixing.

Cross-border M&A

In a study conducted in 2000 by Lehman Brothers, it was found that, on average, large M&A deals cause the domestic currency of the target corporation to appreciate by 1% relative to the acquirer's. For every $1-billion deal, the currency of the target corporation increased in value by 0.5%. More specifically, the report found that in the period immediately after the deal is announced, there is generally a strong upward movement in the target corporation's domestic currency (relative to the acquirer's currency). Fifty days after the announcement, the target currency is then, on average, 1% stronger.

The rise of globalization has exponentially increased the market for cross border M&A. In 1996 alone there were over 2000 cross border transactions worth a total of approximately $256 billion. This rapid increase has taken many M&A firms by surprise because the majority of them never had to consider acquiring the capabilities or skills required to effectively handle this kind of transaction. In the past, the market's lack of significance and a more strictly national mindset prevented the vast majority of small and mid-sized companies from considering cross border intermediation as an option which left M&A firms inexperienced in this field. This same reason also prevented the development of any extensive academic works on the subject.

Due to the complicated nature of cross border M&A, the vast majority of cross border actions have unsuccessful results. Cross border intermediation has many more levels of complexity to it then regular intermediation seeing as corporate governance, the power of the average employee, company regulations, political factors customer expectations, and countries' culture are all crucial factors that could spoil the transaction. Because of such complications, many business brokers are finding the International Corporate Finance Group and organizations like it to be a necessity in M&A today.

BUSINESS VALUATION

Business valuation is a process and a set of procedures used to determine the economic value of an owner's interest in a business. Business valuation is often used to estimate the selling price of a business, resolve disputes related to estate and gift taxation, divorce litigation, allocate business purchase price among the business assets, and many other business and legal disputes.

Fair Market Value

"Fair market value" is defined as the price, expressed in terms of cash equivalents, at which property would change hands between a hypothetical willing and able buyer and a hypothetical willing and able seller, acting at arms length in an open and unrestricted market, when neither is under compulsion to buy or sell and when both have reasonable knowledge of the relevant facts. See IRS Rev. Rul. 59-60, 1959-1, Cum. Bulletin 237, codified at 26 C.F.R. § 20.2031-1(b). The fair market value standard incorporates certain assumptions, including the assumptions that the hypothetical purchaser is reasonably prudent and rational but is not motivated by any synergistic or strategic influences; that the business will continue as a going concern and not be liquidated; that the hypothetical transaction will be conducted in cash or equivalents; and that the parties are willing and able to consummate the transaction. These assumptions might not, and probably do not, reflect the actual conditions of the market in which the subject business might be sold. However, these conditions are assumed because they yield a uniform standard of value, after applying generally-accepted valuation techniques, which allows meaningful comparison between businesses which are similarly situated.

Elements of Business Valuation

Economic Conditions

A business valuation report generally begins with a description of national, regional and local economic conditions existing as of the valuation date, as well as the conditions of the industry in which the subject business operates. A common source of economic information for the first section of the business valuation report is the Federal Reserve Board's Beige Book, published quarterly by the Federal Reserve Bank. State governments and industry associations often publish useful statistics describing regional and industry conditions.

The financial statement analysis generally follows a description of the subject company. One of the first techniques that a business valuation professional applies is called "normalization" of the subject company's financial statements. Normalizing the company's financial statements permits the valuation expert to compare the subject company to other businesses in the same geographic area and industry, and to discover trends affecting the company over time. By comparing a company's financial statements in different time periods, the valuation expert can view growth or decline in revenues or expenses, increases or decreases in assets or liabilities, or other financial trends within the subject company. Valuation professionals also review the subject company's financial ratios, such as the current ratio, quick ratio, and other liquidity ratios; collection ratios; and other measures of a company's financial performance.

Normalization of Financial Statements

The most common normalization adjustments fall into the following four categories:

1. *Comparability Adjustments.* The valuator may adjust the subject company's financial statements to facilitate a comparison between the subject company and other businesses in the same industry or geographic location. These adjustments are intended to eliminate differences between the way that published industry data is presented and the way that the subject company's data is presented in its financial statements.
2. *Non-operating Adjustments.* It is reasonable to assume that if a business were sold in a hypothetical sales transaction (which is the underlying premise of the fair market value standard), the seller would retain any assets which were not related to the production of earnings or price those non-operating assets separately. For this reason, non-operating assets (such as excess cash) are usually eliminated from the balance sheet.

3. *Non-recurring Adjustments.* The subject company's financial statements may be affected by events that are not expected to recur, such as the purchase or sale of assets, a lawsuit, or an unusually large revenue or expense. These non-recurring items are adjusted so that the financial statements will better reflect the management's expectations of future performance.
4. *Discretionary Adjustments.* The owners of private companies may be paid at variance from the market level of compensation that similar executives in the industry might command. In order to determine fair market value, the owner's compensation, benefits, perquisites and distributions must be adjusted to industry standards. Similarly, the rent paid by the subject business for the use of property owned by the company's owners individually may be scrutinized.

Income, Asset and Market Approaches

Three different approaches are commonly used in business valuation: the income approach, the asset-based approach, and the market approach. Within each of these approaches, there are various techniques for determining the fair market value of a business. Generally, the income approaches determine value by calculating the net present value of the benefit stream generated by the business; the asset-based approaches determine value by adding the sum of the parts of the business; and the market approaches determine value by comparing the subject company to other companies in the same industry, of the same size, and/or within the same region. In determining which of these approaches to use, the valuation professional must exercise discretion. Each technique has advantages and drawbacks, which must be considered when applying those techniques to a particular subject company. Most treatises and court decisions encourage the valuator to consider more than one technique, which must be reconciled with each other to arrive at a value conclusion. A measure of common sense and a good grasp of mathematics is helpful.

Income Approaches

The income approaches determine fair market value by multiplying the benefit stream generated by the subject company times a discount or capitalization rate. The discount or capitalization rate converts the stream of benefits into present value. There are several different income approaches, including capitalization of earnings or cash flows, discounted future cash flows ("DCF"), and the excess earnings method (which is a hybrid of asset and income approaches). Most of the income approaches consider the subject company's historical financial data; only the DCF method requires the subject company to provide projected financial data. Most of the income approaches look to the company's adjusted historical financial data for a single period; only DCF requires data for multiple future periods.

The discount or capitalization rate must be matched to the type of benefit stream to which it is applied. The result of a value calculation under the income approach is generally the fair market value of a controlling, marketable interest in the subject company, since the entire benefit stream of the subject company is most often valued, and the capitalization and discount rates are derived from statistics concerning public companies.

Discount or Capitalization Rates

A discount or capitalization rate is used to determine the present value of the expected returns of a business. The discount rate and capitalization rate are closely related to each other, but distinguishable. Generally speaking, the discount rate or capitalization rate may be defined as the yield necessary to attract investors to a particular investment, given the risks associated with that investment. The discount rate is applied only to discounted cash flow (DCF) valuations, which are based on projected business data over multiple periods of time.

In DCF valuations, a series of projected cash flows is divided by the discount rate to derive the present value of the discounted cash flows. The sum of the discounted cash flows is added to a terminal value, which represents the present value of business cash flows into perpetuity. The sum of the discounted cash flows and the terminal value is the value of the business. On the other hand, a capitalization rate is applied in methods of business valuation that are based on historical business data for a single period of time.

The after-tax net cash flow capitalization rate is equal to the discount rate minus the long-term sustainable growth rate. The after-tax net cash flow of a business is divided by the capitalization rate to derive the present value. Capitalization rates may be modified so that they may be applied to after-tax net income or pre-tax cash flows or income.

There are several different methods of determining the appropriate discount rates. The discount rate is composed of two elements:

(1) the risk-free rate, which is the return that an investor would expect from a secure, practically risk-free investment, such as a government bond; plus

(2) a risk premium that compensates an investor for the relative level of risk associated with a particular investment in excess of the risk-free rate. Most importantly, the selected discount or capitalization rate must be consistent with stream of benefits to which it is to be applied.

Build-Up Method

The Build-Up Method is a widely-recognized method of determining the after-tax net cash flow discount rate, which in turn yields the capitalization rate. The figures used in the Build-Up Method are derived from various sources. This method is called a "build-up" method because it is the sum of risks associated with various classes of assets. It is based on the principle that investors would require a greater return on classes of assets that are more risky. The first element of an Build-Up capitalization rate is the risk-free rate, which is the rate of return for long-term government bonds. Investors who buy large-cap equity stocks, which are inherently more risky than long-term government bonds, require a greater return, so the next element of the Build-Up method is the equity risk premium.

In determining a company's value, the long-horizon equity risk premium is used because the Company's life is assumed to be infinite. The sum of the risk-free rate and the equity risk premium yields the long-term average market rate of return on large public company stocks. Similarly, investors who invest in small cap stocks, which are riskier than blue-chip stocks, require a greater return, called the "size premium." Size premium data is generally available from two sources: Ibbotson & Associates' Stocks, Bonds, Bills & Inflation and Duff & Phelps' Risk Premium Report.

By adding the first three elements of a Build-Up discount rate, we can determine the rate of return that investors would require on their investments in small public company stocks. These three elements of the Build-Up discount rate are known collectively as the "systematic risks." In addition to systematic risks, the discount rate must include "unsystematic risks," which fall into two categories. One of those categories is the "industry risk premium." Ibbotson's yearbooks contain empirical data to quantify the risks associated with various industries, grouped by SIC industry code. The other category of unsystematic risk is referred to as "specific company risk." Historically, no published data has been available to quantify specific company risks. However as of late 2006, new research has been able to quantify, or isolate, this risk for publicly-traded stocks through the use of Total Beta calculations.

P. Butler and K. Pinkerton have outlined a procedure using a modified capital asset pricing model (CAPM) to calculate the company specific risk premium. The model uses an equality between the standard CAPM which relies on the total beta on one side of the equation; and the firm's beta, size premium and company specific risk premium on the other. The equality is then solved for the company specific risk premium as the only unknown.

It is important to understand why this capitalization rate for small, privately-held companies is significantly higher than the return that an investor might expect to receive from other common types of investments, such as money market accounts, mutual funds, or even real estate. Those investments involve substantially lower levels of risk than an investment in a closely-held company. Depository accounts are insured by the federal government (up to certain limits); mutual funds are composed of publicly-traded stocks, for which risk can be substantially minimized through portfolio diversification; and real estate almost invariably appreciates in value of long time horizons.

Closely-held companies, on the other hand, frequently fail for a variety of reasons too numerous to name. Examples of the risk can be witnessed in the storefronts on every Main Street in America. There are no federal guarantees. The risk of investing in a private company cannot be reduced through diversification, and most businesses do not own the type of hard assets that can ensure capital appreciation over time. This is why investors demand a much higher return on their investment in closely-held businesses; such investments are inherently much more risky.

Capital Asset Pricing Model ("CAP-M")

The Capital Asset Pricing model is another method of determining the appropriate discount rate in business valuations. The CAP-M method originated from the Nobel Prize winning studies of Harry Markowitz, James Tobin and William Sharpe. Like the Ibbotson Build-Up method, the CAP-M method derives the discount rate by adding a risk premium to the risk-free rate. In this instance, however, the risk premium is derived by multiplying the equity risk premium times "beta," which is a measure of stock price volatility. Beta is published by various sources (including Ibbotson Associates, which was used in this valuation) for particular industries and companies. Beta is associated with the systematic risks of an investment. One of the criticisms of the CAP-M method is that beta is derived from the volatility of prices of publicly-traded companies, which are likely to differ from private companies in their capital structures, diversification of products and markets, access to credit markets, size, management depth, and many other respects. Where private companies can be shown to be sufficiently similar to public companies, however, the CAP-M model may be appropriate.

Weighted Average Cost of Capital ("WACC")

The weighted average cost of capital is the third major approach to determining a discount rate. The WACC method determines the subject company's actual cost of capital by calculating the weighted average of the company's cost of debt and cost of equity. The WACC capitalization rate must be applied to the subject company's net cash flow to invested equity. One of the problems with this method is that the valuator may elect to calculate WACC according to the subject company's existing capital structure, the average industry capital structure, or the optimal capital structure. Such discretion detracts from the objectivity of this approach, in the minds of some critics. Once the capitalization or discount rate is determined, it must be applied to an appropriate benefit streams: pretax cash flow, aftertax cash flow, pretax net income, after tax net income, excess earnings, projected cash flow, etc. The result of this formula is the indicated value before discounts. Before moving on to calculate discounts, however, the valuation professional must consider the indicated value under the asset and market approaches.

Asset Based Approaches

The value of asset based analysis a business is equal to the sum of its parts. That is the theory underlying the asset based approaches to business valuation. The asset approach to business valuation is based on the principle of substitution: no rational investor will pay more for the business assets than the cost of procuring assets of similar economic utility. In contrast to the income based approaches, which require the valuation professional to make subjective judgments about capitalization or discount rates, the adjusted net book value method is relatively objective. Pursuant to accounting convention, most assets are reported on the books of the subject company at their acquisition value, net of depreciation where applicable. These values must be adjusted to fair market value wherever possible.

The value of a company's intangible assets, such as goodwill, is generally impossible to determine apart from the company's overall enterprise value. For this reason, the asset based approach is not the most probative method of determining the value of going business concerns. In these cases, the asset based approach yields a result that is probably lesser than the fair market value of the business. In considering an asset-based approach, the valuation professional must consider whether the shareholder whose interest is being value would have any authority to access the value of the assets directly. Shareholders own shares in a corporation, but not its assets, which are owned by the corporation. A controlling shareholder may have the authority to direct the corporation to sell all or part of the assets it owns and to distribute the proceeds to the shareholder(s).

The non-controlling shareholder, however, lacks this authority and cannot access the value of the assets. As a result, the value of a corporation's assets is rarely the most relevant indicator of value to a shareholder who cannot avail himself of that value. Adjusted net book value may be the most relevant standard of value where liquidation is imminent or ongoing; where a company earnings or cash flow are nominal, negative or worth less than its assets; or where net book value is standard in the industry in which the company operates. None of these situations applies to the Company which is the subject of this valuation report. However, the adjusted net book value may be used as a "sanity check" when compared to other methods of valuation, such as the income and market approaches.

Market Approaches

The market approach to business valuation is rooted in the economic principle of competition: that in a free market the supply and demand forces will drive the price of business assets to a certain equilibrium. Buyers would not pay more for the business, and the sellers will not accept less, than the price of a comparable business enterprise. It is similar in many respects to the "comparable sales" method that is commonly used in real estate appraisal. The market price of the stocks of publicly traded companies engaged in the same or a similar line of business, whose shares are actively traded in a free and open market, can be a valid indicator of value when the transactions in which stocks are traded are sufficiently similar to permit meaningful comparison. The difficulty lies in identifying public companies that are sufficiently comparable to the subject company for this purpose. Also, as for a private company, the equity is less liquid (in other words its stocks are less easy to buy or sell) than for a public company, its value is considered to be slightly lower than such a market-based valuation would give.

Guideline Public Company Method

The Guideline Public Company method entails a comparison of the subject company to publicly-traded companies. The comparison is generally based on published data regarding the public companies' stock price and earnings, sales, or revenues, which is expressed as a fraction known as a "multiple." If the guideline public companies are sufficiently similar to each other and the subject company to permit a meaningful comparison, then their multiples should be nearly equal. The public companies identified for comparison purposes should be similar to the subject company in terms of industry, product lines, market, growth, and risk. In another variation of this method, the valuator may determine market multiples by reviewing published data regarding actual transactions involving either minority or controlling interests in either publicly traded or closely held companies. In judging whether a reasonable basis for comparison exists, the valuator must consider:

(1) the similarity of qualitative and quantitative investment and investor characteristics;

(2) the extent to which reliable data is known about the transactions in which interests in the guideline companies were bought and sold; and

(3) whether or not the price paid for the guideline companies was in an arms-length transaction, or a forced or distressed sale.

To identify guideline companies that might be comparable to the Company that is the subject of this valuation report, we reviewed data provided by the Center for Economic and Industry Research, a service affiliated with the National Association of Certified Valuation Analysts. The data was compiled by BIZCOMPS and Multex, two widely-used providers of data.

Discounts and Premiums

The valuation approaches yield the fair market value of the Company as a whole. In valuing a minority, non-controlling interest in a business, however, the valuation professional must consider the applicability of discounts that affect such interests. Discussions of discounts and premiums frequently begin with a review of the "levels of value." There are three common levels of value: controlling interest, marketable minority, and non-marketable minority. The intermediate level, marketable minority interest, is lesser than the controlling interest level and higher than the non-marketable minority interest level. The marketable minority interest level represents the perceived value of equity interests that are freely traded without any restrictions.

These interests are generally traded on the New York Stock Exchange, AMEX, NASDAQ, and other exchanges where there is a ready market for equity securities. These values represent a minority interest in the subject companies-small blocks of stock that represent less than 50% of the company's equity, and usually much less than 50%. Controlling interest level is the value that an investor would be willing to pay to acquire more than 50% of a company's stock, thereby gaining the attendant prerogatives of control. Some of the prerogatives of control include: electing directors, hiring and firing the company's management and determining their compensation; declaring dividends and distributions, determining the company's strategy and line of business, and acquiring, selling or liquidating the business. This level of value generally contains a control premium over the intermediate level of value, which typically ranges from 25% to 50%. An additional premium may be paid by strategic investors who are motivated by synergistic motives.

Non-marketable, minority level is the lowest level on the chart, representing the level at which non-controlling equity interests in private companies are generally valued or traded. This level of value is discounted because no ready market exists in which to purchase or sell interests. Private companies are less "liquid" than publicly-traded companies, and transactions in private companies take longer and are more uncertain. Between the intermediate and lowest levels of the chart, there are restricted shares of publicly-traded companies. Despite a growing inclination of the IRS and Tax Courts to challenge valuation discounts, Shannon Pratt suggested in a scholarly presentation recently that valuation discounts are actually increasing as the differences between public and private companies is widening. Publicly-traded stocks have grown more liquid in the past decade due to rapid electronic trading, reduced commissions, and governmental deregulation. These developments have not improved the liquidity of interests in private companies, however. Valuation discounts are multiplicative, so they must be considered in order. Control premiums and their inverse, minority interest discounts, are considered before marketability discounts are applied.

Discount for Lack of Control

The first discount that must be considered is the discount for lack of control, which in this instance is also a minority interest discount. Minority interest discounts are the inverse of control premiums, to which the following mathematical relationship exists: $MID = 1 - [1 / (1 + CP)]$ The most common source of data regarding control premiums is the Control Premium Study, published annually by Mergerstat since 1972. Mergerstat compiles data regarding publicly announced mergers, acquisitions and divestitures involving 10% or more of the equity interests in public companies, where the purchase price is $1 million or more and at least one of the parties to the transaction is a U.S. entity. Mergerstat defines the "control premium" as the percentage difference between the acquisition price and the share price of the freely-traded public shares five days prior to the announcement of the M&A transaction. While it is not without valid criticism, Mergerstat control premium data (and the minority interest discount derived therefrom) is widely accepted within the valuation profession.

Discount for Lack of Marketability

Another factor to be considered in valuing closely held companies is the marketability of an interest in such businesses. Marketability is defined as the ability to convert the business interest into cash quickly, with minimum transaction and administrative costs, and with a high degree of certainty as to the amount of net proceeds. There is usually a cost and a time lag associated with locating interested and capable buyers of interests in privately-held companies, because there is no established market of readily-available buyers and sellers. All other factors being equal, an interest in a publicly traded company is worth more because it is readily marketable. Conversely, an interest in a private-held company is worth less because no established market exists. The IRS Valuation Guide for Income, Estate and Gift Taxes, Valuation Training for Appeals Officers acknowledges the relationship between value and marketability, stating: "Investors prefer an asset which is easy to sell, that is, liquid."

The discount for lack of control is separate and distinguishable from the discount for lack of marketability. It is the valuation professional's task to quantify the lack of marketability of an interest in a privately-held company. Because, in this case, the subject interest is not a controlling interest in the Company, and the owner of that interest cannot compel liquidation to convert the subject interest to cash quickly, and no established market exists on which that interest could be sold, the discount for lack of marketability is appropriate. Several empirical studies have been published that attempt to quantify the discount for lack of marketability. These studies include the restricted stock studies and the pre-IPO studies. The aggregate of these studies indicate average discounts of 35% and 50%, respectively. Some experts believe the Lack of Control and Marketabilty discouts can aggregate discounts for as much as ninety percent of a Company's fair market value, specifically with family owned companies.

Restricted Stock Studies

Restricted stocks are equity securities of public companies that are similar in all respects to the freely traded stocks of those companies except that they carry a restriction that prevents them from being traded on the open market for a certain period of time, which is usually one year (two years prior to 1990). This restriction from active trading, which amounts to a lack of marketability, is the only distinction between the restricted stock and its freely-traded counterpart. Restricted stock can be traded in private transactions and usually do so at a discount. The restricted stock studies attempt to verify the difference in price at which the restricted shares trade versus the price at which the same unrestricted securities trade in the open market as of the same date. The underlying data by which these studies arrived at their conclusions has not been made public. Consequently, it is not possible when valuing a particular company to compare the characteristics of that company to the study data. Still, the existence of a marketability discount has been recognized by valuation professionals and the Courts, and the restricted stock studies are frequently cited as empirical evidence. Notably, the lowest average discount reported by these studies was 26% and the highest average discount was 45%.

Option Pricing

In addition to the restricted stock studies, U.S. publicly traded companies are able to sell stock to offshore investors (SEC Regulation S, enacted in 1990) without registering the shares with the Securities and Exchange Commission. The offshore buyers may resell these shares in the United States, still without having to register the shares, after holding them for just 40 days. Typically, these shares are sold for 20% to 30% below the publicly traded share price. Some of these transactions have been reported with discounts of more than 30%, resulting from the lack of marketability. These discounts are similar to the marketability discounts inferred from the restricted and pre-IPO studies, despite the holding period being just 40 days. Studies based on the prices paid for options have also confirmed similar discounts. If one holds restricted stock and purchases an option to sell that stock at the market price (a put), the holder has, in effect, purchased marketability for the shares. The price of the put is equal to the marketability discount. The range of marketability discounts derived by this study was 32% to 49%.

Pre-IPO Studies

Another approach to measure the marketability discount is to compare the prices of stock offered in initial public offerings (IPOs) to transactions in the same company's stocks prior to the IPO. Companies that are going public are required to disclose all transactions in their stocks for a period of three years prior to the IPO. The pre-IPO studies are the leading alternative to the restricted stock stocks in quantifying the marketability discount. The pre-IPO studies are sometimes criticized because the sample size is relatively small, the pre-IPO transactions may not be arm's length, and the financial structure and product lines of the studied companies may have changed during the three year pre-IPO window.

Applying the Studies

The studies confirm what the marketplace knows intuitively: Investors covet liquidity and loathe obstacles that impair liquidity. Prudent investors buy illiquid investments only when there is a sufficient discount in the price to increase the rate of return to a level which brings risk-reward back into balance. The referenced studies establish a reasonable range of valuation discounts from the mid-30%s to the low 50%s. The more recent studies appeared to yield a more conservative range of discounts than older studies, which may have suffered from smaller sample sizes. Other methods of quantifying the lack of marketability discount, such as the Quantifying Marketability Discounts Model (QMDM) have not been considered and are beyond the scope of this report.

VIABLE SYSTEM MODEL

The Viable Systems Model, or VSM is a model of the organisational structure of any viable or autonomous system. A viable system is any system organised in such a way as to meet the demands of surviving in the changing environment. One of the prime features of systems that survive is that they are adaptable. The VSM expresses a model for a viable system, which is an abstracted cybernetic description that is applicable to any organisation that is a viable system and capable of autonomy.

Overview

The model was developed by operations research theorist and cybernetician Stafford Beer in his book Brain of the Firm (1972). Together with Beer's earlier works on cybernetics applied to management, this book effectively founded management cybernetics.

The first thing to note about the cybernetic theory of organisations encapsulated in the VSM is that viable systems are recursive; viable systems contain viable systems that can be modelled using an identical cybernetic description as the higher (and lower) level systems in the containment hierarchy (Beer expresses this property of viable systems as cybernetic isomorphism).

Components of the Viable System Model

Here we give a brief introduction to the cybernetic description of the organisation encapsulated in a single level of the VSM.

A viable system is composed of five interacting subsystems which may be mapped onto aspects of organisational structure. In broad terms Systems 1-3 are concerned with the 'here and now' of the organisation's operations, System 4 is concerned with the 'there and then'-strategical responses to the effects of external, environmental and future demands on the organisation. System 5 is concerned with balancing the 'here and now' and the 'there and then' to give policy directives which maintain the organisation as a viable entity

- System 1 in a viable system contains several primary activities. Each System 1 primary activity is itself a viable system due to the recursive nature of systems as described above. These are concerned with performing a function that implements at least part of the key transformation of the organisation.

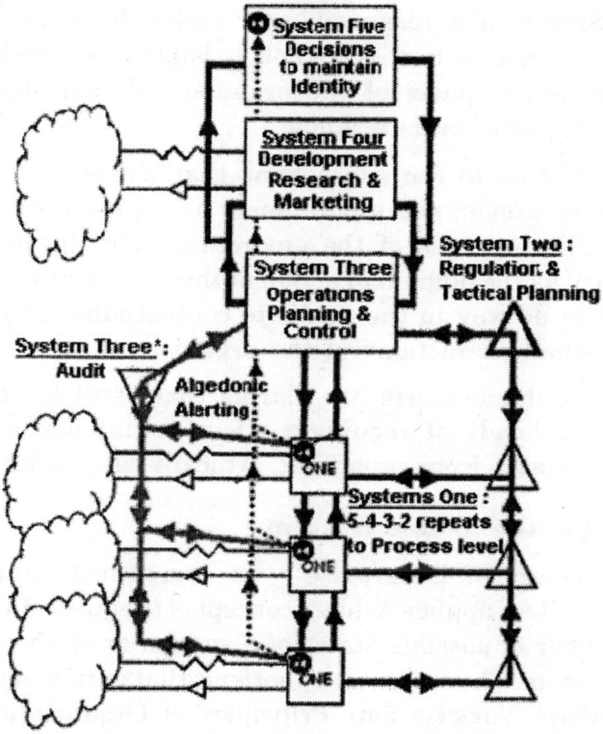

Principle functions of the VSM

- System 2 represents the information channels and bodies that allow the primary activities in System 1 to communicate between each other and which allow System 3 to monitor and co-ordinate the activities within System 1.
- System 3 represents the structures and controls that are put into place to establish the rules, resources, rights and responsibilities of System 1 and to provide an interface with Systems 4/5.

- System 4-The bodies that make up System 4 are responsible for looking outwards to the environment to monitor how the organisation needs to adapt to remain viable.
- System 5 is responsible for policy decisions within the organisation as a whole to balance demands from different parts of the organisation and steer the organisation as a whole.

In addition to the subsystems that make up the first level of recursion, the environment is represented in the model. The presence of the environment in the model is necessary as the domain of action of the system and without it there is no way in the model to contextualise or ground the internal interactions of the organisation.

- Algedonic Alerts are alarms that escalate through the levels of recursion when actual performance deviates from capability, typically after a time out.

Rules for the Viable System

In "Heart of Enterprise" a companion volume to "Brain...", Beer applies Ashby's concept of (Requisite) Variety: the number of possible states of a system or of an element of the system. There are two aphorisms that permit observers to calculate Variety; four Principles of Organization; the Recursive System Theorem; three Axioms of Management and a Law of Cohesion. These rules ensure the Requisite Variety condition is satisfied, in effect that resources are matched to requirement.

Regulatory Aphorisms

These aphorisms are:

- It is not necessary to enter the black box to understand the nature of the function it performs.
- It is not necessary to enter the black box to calculate the variety that it potentially may generate.

Principles of Organisation

(Principles are 'primary sources of particular outcome')

These principles are:

- Managerial, operational and environmental varieties diffusing through an institutional system, tend to equate; they should be designed to do so with minimum damage to people and cost.
- The four directional channels carrying information between the management unit, the operation, and the environment must each have a higher capacity to transmit a given amount of information relevant to variety selection in a given time than the originating subsystem has to generate it in that time.
- Wherever the information carried on a channel capable of distinguishing a given variety crosses a boundary, it undergoes transduction; the variety of the transducer must be at least equivalent to the variety of the channel.
- The operation of the first three principles must be cyclically maintained through time without hiatus or lags.

Recursive System Theorem

This theorem states:

- In a recursive organizational structure any viable system contains, and is contained in, a viable system.

Axioms

(Axioms are statements 'worthy of belief')

These axioms are:

- The sum of horizontal variety disposed by n operational elements (systems one) equals the sum of the vertical variety disposed by the six vertical components of corporate cohesion (5, 4, 3, 3*, 2, 1).

- The variety disposed by System Three resulting from the operation of the First Axiom equals the variety disposed by System Four.
- The variety disposed by System Five equals the residual variety generated by the operation of the Second Axiom.

The Law of Cohesion for Multiple Recursions of the Viable System

This law ('something invariant in nature') states:

- The System One variety accessible to System Three of recursion x equals the variety disposed by the sum of the metasystem of recursion y for every recursive pair.

Measuring Performance

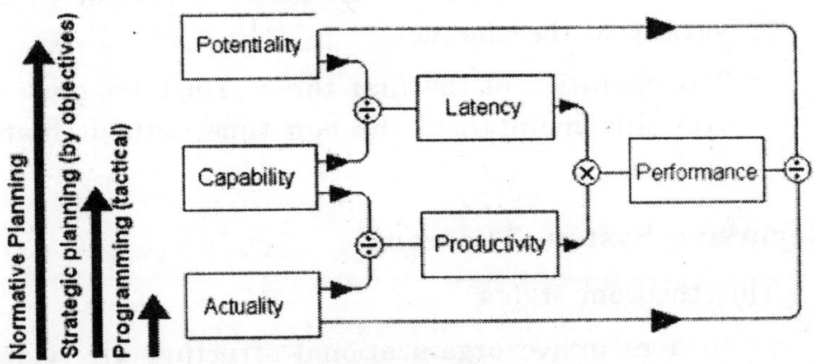

Three measures of capacity producing three measures of achievement

In "Brain..." (p.163) Beer describes a triple vector to characterize activity in a System 1.

The components are:

Actuality: "What we are managing to do now, with existing resources, under existing constraints."

Capability: "This is what we could be doing (still right now) with existing resources, under existing constraints, if we really worked at it."

Potentiality: "This is what we ought to be doing by developing our resources and removing constraints, although still operating within the bounds of what is already known to be feasible."

Beer adds "It would help a lot to fix these definitions clearly in the mind." System 4's job is essentially to realize potential.

He then defines productivity: is the ratio of actuality and capability;

Latency: is the ratio of capability and potentiality;

Performance: is the ratio of actuality and potentiality, and also the product of latency and productivity.

Consider the management of a process with cash earnings or savings for a company or government: potentially £100,000 but aiming to make £ 60,000. Actually sales, savings or taxes of £40,000 are realized.

So potentiality = £100,000; capability = £60,000; actuality = £40,000.

Thus latency = 80/100 = 0.6;

productivity = 40/60 = 0.67;

performance = 0.6 x 0.67= 0.4 (or actuality/potential 40/100).

These methods (also known as normalisations) can be similarly applied in general e.g. to hours worked in the performance of tasks or products in a production process of some kind.

When actuality deviates from capability, because someone did something well or something badly, an algedonic alert is sent to management. If corrective action, adoption of a good technique or correction of an error, is not taken in a timely manner the alert is escalated. Because the criteria are applied in an ordered hierarchy the management itself need not be, but the routine response functions must be ordered to reflect best known heuristic practice. These heuristics are constantly monitored for improvement by the organization's System 4s.

Pay structures reflect these constraints on performance when capability or potential is realized with, for example, productivity bonuses, stakeholder agreements and intellectual property rights.

Metalanguage

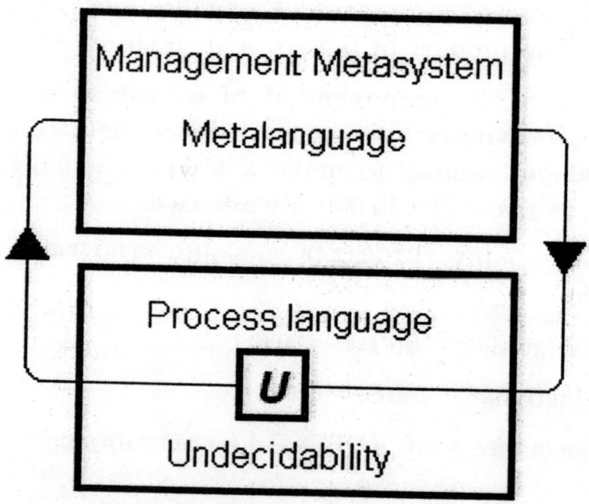

Resolving undecidability by raising the metalanguage

In ascending the recursions of the viable system the context of each autonomous 5-4-3-2 metasystem enlarges and acquires more variety.

This defines a metalanguage stack of increasing capability to resolve undecidability in the autonomous lower levels. If someone near process level needs to innovate to achieve potential, or restore capability help can be secured from management of higher variety.

An algedonic alert, sent when actuality deviates by some statistically significant amount from capability, makes this process automatic.

The notion of adding more variety or states to resolve ambiguity or undecidability (also known as the decision problem) is the subject of Chaitin's metamathmatical conjecture algorithmic information theory and provides a potentially rigorous theoretical basis for a general management heuristic. If a process is not producing the agreed product more information, if applicable, will correct this, resolve ambiguity, conflict or undecidability.

In "Platform for Change" (Beer 1975) the thesis is developed via a collection of papers to learned bodies, including UK Police and Hospitals, to produce a visualization of the "Total System". Here a "relevant ethic" evolves from "experimental ethics" and the "ethic with a busted gut" to produce a sustainable earth with reformed "old institutions" becoming "new institutions" driven by approval (eudemonic criteria "Questions of Metric" in Platform... pp 163-179) from the "software milieu" while culture adopts the systems approach and "Homo Faber" (man the maker) becomes "Homo Gubernator" (self-steering).

BIBLIOGRAPHY

Adelberg, Edward A.: *Papers on Bacterial Genetics*, Boston, Brown and Company, 1960.

Angel, Bradley: *Toxic Threat to Indian Lands: A Greenpeace Report*, San Francisco, Greenpeace, 1991.

Baker, S. H.: *Character Building Clubs for Boys. The Scientific Management of Clubs for Boys*, London, YMCA Boys Department, 1919.

Barnum, Susan R.: *Biotechnology: An Introduction*, Belmont, Thomson/Brooks/Cole, 2005.

Burch, William R. Jr.: *Human Ecology: An Environmental Approach*, Belmont, Duxbury Press, 1994.

Campbell, R. R., and Wade, J. L.: *Society and Environment: The Coming Collision*, Boston, Allyn and Bacon, 1972.

Carey, W.: *Public Opinion and the Communication of Consent,* New York: Guilford Publications, 1995.

Chrispeels, Maarten : *Plants, Genes and Crop Biotechnology*, Sudbury MA, Jones and Barlett Publishers, 2003.

Cox, Earl D. : *Beyond Humanity: Cyber Evolution and Future Minds*, Roackland, Charles River Media, 1996.

Daubenmire, R. F.: *Plants and Environment*, New York, Wiley, 1947.

David Sadava: *Plants, Genes and Crop Biotechnology*, Sudbury MA, Jones and Barlett Publishers, 2003.

Dixon, Dougal: *After Man-A Zoology of the Future*, New York, St. Martin's Press, 1981.

Dodds, John H.: *Plant Genetic Engineering*, New York, Cambridge University Press, 1985.

Edwards-Rees, D.: *The Service of Youth Book*, Wallington, Religious Education Press, 1943.

Gitman, Lawrence J.: *Principles of Managerial Finance*, MA: Addison Wesley Longman, 2000.

Hill, David: *The Quality of Life in America; Pollution, Poverty, Power, and Fear*, New York, Holt, Rinehart and Winston, 1973.

Johnson, Hazel: *Financial Institutions and Markets: A Global Perspective*, NY, McGraw Hill, 1993.

Kruvant, W.J.: *People, Energy, and Pollution*, Cambridge, Ballinger Publishing, 1975.

Martin, Justin: *The Man Behind Money*, Perseus Book Group, 2000.

Matthews, J. E.: *Working with Youth Groups*, London, University of London Press, 1966.

Milson, F.: *Growing With the Job*, London, National Assocation of Youth Clubs, 1968.

Petty, Keown, Scott, and Martin: *Basic Financial Management*, Prentice Hall, 1993.

Primrose, S.B.: *Principles of Gene Manipulation*, London, Blackwell Scientific Publications, 1989.

Rifkin, Jeremy: *The Biotech Century*, New York, Penguin Putnam, 1998

Schall and Haley: *Introduction to Financial Management*, McGraw-hill, 1988.

Vallette, J.: *The International Trade in Wastes: A Greenpeace Inventory*, Washington, Greenpeace, 1989.

Walden, Richard: *Genetic Transformation in Plants*, England, Open University Press, 1988.

Zupan, J.M.: *The Distribution of Air Quality in the New York Region*, Baltimore, Johns Hopkins University Press, 1973.

INDEX

G

H

I

L

M

□□□